GO MANIFEST YOURSELF!

YOURSELF!

An Abundantly Abundant Mindset

By D.R. Riley

Printed in the United States of America

Riley, D.R.
Go Manifest Yourself!: An Abundantly Abundant Mindset

For more information on reproducing sections of this book or sales
of this book, go to www.tormentpublishing.com

Contents:

Chapter 1: Woo Woo and Reality

The Law of Attraction, ugh! This is basically the Law of Stealing with the way it's being taught today. You can't *wish* things into your life. You might as well steal them, because attraction without action is just want. Wanting something leads to wanting to want stuff. Period. (I will get into the evil trap of 'want' later in this book.)

Okay, now that I got that off my chest, let's focus on what an abundant mindset is and how it affects people.

We've all read about positive thinking and how it shapes your life. Well, this is true to a point, but being positive in an environment of negative people will only piss already angry people off. So, this alone will not bring you the fulfillment you desire.

Abundance is an aftereffect of mindset with action. Reality is bound by your actions and intentions. What this means is you make your own reality by populating your existence with the puzzle pieces. Now life is not simple, and if it was simple we would all be perfect at it. Perfect is just boring, and we are not living this existence to sit around and twiddle our thumbs in perpetual bliss. Our existence is our own, and we can choose to experience whatever we want, whenever we want. Culture and society can limit what we experience, but only if you allow it to.

Now this gets me to the point where everyone thinks if you are born in a third-world country you are screwed. But this is not the case, because your priorities and what makes you feel abundant and happy is different depending on the life you started with. Not everyone desires endless riches and a mansion on top of a hill. For some people, that has never crossed their mind. For those people it's about the experiences and the creative love that they can take part in. Priorities can change and anyone can desire something different at any moment—and that is a wonderful part of this existence!

When I was younger, I was a massive overthinker. I would worry about what everyone was thinking and whether it was about me or about the situation I was taking part in. This state of mind is a perfect example of how reality works. I chose to turn my focus on what I wanted to do rather than what everyone else was doing. This change in mindset altered my reality almost overnight. I found that people were drawn to me and life became more enjoyable. At the time, I didn't see it, but now it makes perfect sense. We all have the power to perceive the world as we see fit. This one aspect alone can alter reality for your current conscious moment. (I will dig more into actions and reactions later in this book.)

You probably bought this book because of my awesome title! Sure, I was making a pun about abundance, but abundance is the glue to our existence. You can be abundantly happy, wealthy, loved, fed, provided for, satisfied, sought out, famous, and so on. Filling your life with abundance gives life meaning. Without it, we would live in a pointless void. (Abundant void?)

One other area of "woo woo" thinking that you've heard about is collective consciousness and how everything is connected. String theory and quantum entanglement are both turning out to connect to collective consciousness, and therefore validating it to a degree. For me, it is very simple: everything is connected. *Everything.* Everything affects our existence in some way. Just because something sounds "new age" or is talked about around a drum circle doesn't mean that it's just theory or fantasy. This book will help you understand the universal strings that make everything work.

So, just with the little you've read of this chapter so far, you can see that our reality is flexible from multiple angles. There is not one true path to an abundant mindset. Reality is complex and pliable. There are many ways to improve your existence. Mastering one or all of them is up to you.

Now, let's get into the nitty gritty details of each of them so you can instantly increase the abundance and happiness in your life.

So, what do successful and not-miserable people have in common trait-wise? What's that mystery cosmic glue that binds their lives together and brings them the things they want? We're in luck. Psychologists and others have figured out many of the mental traits these people share, and they're not as "woo-woo" as others would have you think.

These are mental traits that *lead* to action, which is the real driving force behind bringing more abundance to our lives. The Law of Attraction and the fact that everything in the universe is connected both come into play here. It boils down to having the right mindset that will encourage you to take the actions that will bring abundance into your life—whether it be more money, love, happiness, or good health.

But you have to start somewhere, so I suppose it's time to compare this to something in real life.

Think of these mental traits as your training wheels. You start out riding that little kid's bike when you're five years old, doing circles in your driveway (while your parents record you so they can embarrass you in front of your first date). This is a necessary first step: you must get used to the *idea* of riding your own bike before you can ride your own bike. See yourself doing it even if you're still using dorky training wheels. Then you can take the actions that will bring more fun, happiness, and joy to your life.

Once you feel confident enough, you *act*. You ride your bike down the street, meet new friends, go to the park, and maybe even go to the candy store. You might face-plant a few times, but it sure beats staying in the driveway dreaming about the places you could go. Many people never ride their bikes out of the driveway—or even leave their porch—for their entire lives. You don't want to do that, do you?

And if you want to stay in the house, why did you pick up this book?

Chapter 2: The Training Wheels
Seven Mental Traits of Happy, Successful People

1) They crave big adventures and shun boredom.

As soon as you ride your bike in circles, you imagine the places you can go once you get those training wheels off (and that ugly basket that came attached to your bike, too). You see older kids setting up ramps in the streets, doing wheelies, and racing each other. They're having a blast and you want an abundance of fun, too, even if you fall and scrape your knees. You want out of the box that is your driveway where the big adventures await!

But your little brother doesn't want to leave the driveway, and seems content to just ride his bike in circles forever, always taking care to avoid scratching your dad's expensive SUV. The second you get your training wheels off, you ride your bike out to that makeshift ramp, pedal as fast as you can, jump it, and fall off your bike like an idiot. To top it off, you get your shoelaces caught in the bike chain. (Remember that fiasco?) Your little brother laughs, but you're having fun. You try again and make a perfect landing, then wave your brother out to have fun, too.

But he refuses and keeps pedaling in a circle. He likes to stay in his safe, boring box (the driveway). While he keeps circling on a slab of concrete only fifteen feet wide, you ride off with your new friends, and it turns out they don't care that you tangled your shoelaces in the bike chain, because all of them once did it, too.

2) They realize it's all out there for the taking.

Let's get off the bicycles for now and move on to the dating scene. An abundance of love is something everyone wants more of, right? Unless you hate all people, you've made several attempts in the dating scene.

Let's take Stan. Stan is angry that he can't get a date using his favorite online service. He's been trying for months, and a few women have messaged him, but all of his first dates have ended with no follow-up. To cope, Stan sends angry emails to the women who have rebuffed him, calling them names and just being an unpleasant jerk. He decides there's no one out there for him, and instead of trying again, he joins a forum of similar, frustrated men who believe the same. He now spends his time bathing in the same misery he tried to give out.

Jerry knows The One is out there. He refuses to believe otherwise. He only has to find her. Though he has had little luck with online dating, one day he sits next to a beautiful young woman on the bus who has just adopted a kitten. A fellow cat lover, Jerry strikes up a conversation. As the two talk more and realize they both enjoy fostering cats, he gets up the courage to ask her out on a date. She accepts! Two years later, the two marry and start a rescue operation for abandoned cats.

3) They decide today's the time to feel joy and give back instead of resenting others' happiness.

Successful, abundant people know how to count their blessings rather than dwelling on everything that's wrong with their lives.

We've all seen the following drama play out online: someone has seen good success and shares their fortune with the world, handing out advice as a way to give back. For example, Mary writes a blog about how she lost her first fifteen pounds on her diet journey. Though she still has a hundred pounds to lose, she grabs onto the growing abundance of her health rather than resenting the progress she still has to make. The Law of Attraction works once again here—Mary's blog and upbeat attitude brings her encouragement from her readers, which further convinces her to stick with her diet and reach a healthy weight.

Stan is still miserable and has struggled for years to lose weight. He's only lost ten pounds in the past year and his diet is hard. He writes a blog bemoaning this. He calls those who have lost weight anorexics and liars. It's impossible to lose weight, he says, which brings a wave of readers who agree and reinforce Stan's belief. Stan realizes he was right and gives up trying to improve his health. By refusing to see the progress he's made, he's only attracted more misery.

4) They know change can be good. Instead of fearing it, they dive in.

I hated moving as a kid because I had to change schools once every few years. Just when I'd made a few decent friends, my family would pack up and move yet again.

Junior high was the longest I stayed in one school system. After a rough few years dealing with other junior high kids, we wound up having to move yet again, and, of course, it was to another school district. After making lots of friends, I was saddened. I had just started high school in this district and my social life was no longer a disaster.

It was rough at first, being in a new high school, but soon after moving to the new district, I got over my sadness and made new friends. It so happened that I sat down next to a girl on the bus one morning. Instead of staying to myself as I usually did, I struck up a conversation.

I still have that friend many years later.

5) They take actions to shape their lives rather than just waiting and reacting to what happens.

Most successful people you've heard about (movie stars, singers, businesspeople, scientists, etc.) weren't just dropped into their current lives by aliens or by finding a magical genie. (That would be nice if it could happen to you or me, right?)

Sure, there are exceptions. Some people are lucky enough to be born to famous parents. Others have the wealth to make things happen more easily for them. But in most cases, these people started at the bottom, just like you and me.

They knew they could get to where they wanted, but *only if they did the work*. None of these people waited for someone to hand their dreams, happiness, or money to them on a platter. Think of the aspiring actor who gets in his ancient Toyota and drives to Hollywood, or the university graduate who put herself through school by flipping burgers.

Okay, so that last one isn't very realistic. A fast food job won't pay for tuition, but the point is that *these people acted*. They weren't content with dreaming.

6) They're willing to learn and don't pretend they know everything.

Everybody's met at least one "know-it-all" in their life. Don't be that person, and if *you* are that person, stop being that person.

Everyone has more to learn. Yes, *everybody*. It's a big, interconnected universe out there, and even the whole of humanity doesn't know even a fraction of a percent of everything there is to learn in all of existence. Some find this idea terrifying, but those who are willing to learn new things have a leg up.

For years, I struggled to lose the extra weight that had piled on over the years. While it was never severe, it was getting that way. I made many tries to clean up my eating by sticking with the conventional advice of eating a grain-based diet. I'd be able to stick with these eating habits for a while, but little weight would come off, and overall I found the numbers were going higher as the years passed. For most of that time I believed (as many do) that it was my fault I wasn't making any progress.

But then I dug deeper into the problem and learn more about metabolism and healthy eating. I wanted to learn what the non-mainstream had to say and see if any of it would work for me. That's when I learned that some people have done well with losing weight by *cutting* grains. I took the new information, tried it, and reached a normal weight within months. Had I not sought new information and stuck only with what I "knew", I would not be in a good place today.

7) *They're willing to examine if something's not working, and will take steps to find something that does.*

There's an old saying out there: *"Madness is trying the same thing and expecting different results."* Yeah, it's something you've heard your boss say in a boring meeting. I have, too. While my old employer never stuck with those words and refused to take off their training wheels in various situations, this mindset can lead to powerful results if acted upon.

A perfect example of this would be the story of an indie video game programmer who we'll call S. For years, S made cute, family-friendly indie games, but each game failed to find much of an audience and garnered only miserable reviews from critics. S was heartbroken and almost gave up programming games.

But then he decided that maybe something different was what people wanted. Instead of blaming luck, S changed his focus and tried something new, and so he created a horror game.

His horror game was a sensation on the Internet, spawning several sequels, hundreds of rabid fan theories, a popular book series, and even stuffed toys I've seen in claw machines.

An Abundance of Abundance! The Power Ups.

Wow, what a section heading. Catchy, huh? When people think of the word "abundance" they may think of money—namely of swimming in a room full of gold coins or dollar bills. That reminds me of a cartoon I used to watch as a kid.

In reality, there are several types of abundance just waiting to be channeled. Several kinds you may not have thought of can act as power-ups to your plans and actions, helping to bring the more materialistic types of abundance into your life. That's the goal, right?

Health is #1

I'll wave that dorky, styrofoam hand with the #1 printed on it all I want here. Think about it— without your health, how can you enjoy the abundance of anything else, including money? If you're dragging an oxygen tank along with you all the time or are suffering from a poor diet, your lack of health will not motivate you to find an abundance of fun, friends, and love. Who wants to go out when they're lying on the couch with no energy? I don't. I want to lie on the couch!

Brainpower

Being able to figure out how to set your plans in action, and coming up with creative solutions to get you there, is also a valuable power-up. Say you're thinking about starting up your own online business instead of working in a dead-end fast food job for the rest of your life. Your goal is to attract more money and happiness into your life, and you decide the best way is to give people something they've always wanted: a robot that cleans their house and does their laundry. By giving busy working people something they need, you'll convince them to give you their money (see the Law of Attraction working here?). By extension, you'll bring an abundance of money, and likely happiness, into your life.

Inventing this robot will take considerable brainpower, studying the market to find your niche, and coming up with ways to offer something that no one has done before. Much of this ties into the power-up below, and also depends on the first one we discussed—your health. As a writer myself, who must use my brain for eight or nine hours a day, I can attest to the power of a healthy diet on my ability to think and focus, but I'll talk more about this later.

Knowledge

A product of brainpower, knowledge comes from applying the gray matter between your ears, testing things, and learning about what might work best for your plans to bring more abundance into your life. Perhaps you had to learn *who* would buy your house-cleaning robot before setting your plan in motion. You and your team also had to learn mathematics, engineering, and even computer programming before coming up with the concept for your robot. Or, if you're not doing everything yourself, you had to learn how to be nice to people who can make your idea happen. That brings us to the fourth great power-up.

Your Conscience/Ethics

Don't be an a-hole and lie, steal, and cheat on people. Deciding to not pay your business partners enough for their part in creating your amazing robot will only land you in court before a judge and saddle you with legal fees. (Hardly the way to attract an abundance of money into your life, right?) By cheating and stealing, you've only attracted lawyers, who are all too happy to take your money. Some would call this karma, or justice served.

Unethical stuff happens in every occupation, including mine. What awful things can writers do? A lot, actually. I've seen authors get banned from selling on certain online stores because they stuffed their books with nonsensical material to earn more money, and others lose all their customer reviews, which turned out to be paid fakes. Those people may have brought a temporary abundance of cash into their lives only to have it taken away for their actions.

On a more positive note, I've seen many ethical authors and other creatives make a living wage—and stick to it—through years of hard, honest work. While setbacks happen, and don't always happen fairly, these people can often fix things.

Guts

Also known as courage, you'll need an abundance of this if you want to go anywhere with your goals, whether it's finding the love of your life, starting a new career that will make you happier, or making more friends. Putting yourself out there in front of new people is not for the faint of heart, nor is leaving your secure job for an uncertain future. I've seen many people remain in jobs they hate due to fear of the unknown, or remain in loveless relationships, or fail to have much of a social life. There's a reason all those motivational posters you see online show people hang gliding, hiking into the wilderness, or jumping off cliffs into the ocean.

You don't have to jump off a cliff to have guts. I don't recommend it. It can be as simple as going on that date with your crush or as simple as handing in your resignation to your crappy boss.

And without an abundance of guts, you'll never do these things.

A Good Attitude

We've all seen the guy who says, "I can never do that. I'm too tired/not attractive enough/can't leave this office job." And you know what? He's right. With a poor attitude, this poor guy will attract plenty of failure, loneliness, and boredom into his life. Not the abundance you want, right? I've met plenty of people with just this attitude, and their lives always shape up as they say.

Reprogramming yourself to have the coveted "I can do it" attitude will drastically level-up your ability to attract what you want into your life. While it's no guarantee of success, I've never seen anyone without it go very far in life.

Not Being Impatient

Overnight success in any endeavor *can* happen, but its rarity is on par with that of, say, all the planets aligning at once. Every successful singer, celebrity, businessperson, and athlete I can think of put in years of work to get where they are today. They had enough patience with their journey to attract success in the long run. This applies to us regular people, too. Unless you're lucky and have great connections, it took years of promotions, hard work, and perseverance to reach your pay grade. Had you given up after dating a couple of lousy people, would you have met your great significant other? These are just a few examples of how patience can pay off. There's nothing too "woo woo" about this at all.

We'll go into more depth about these concepts in the following chapters, as well as practical ways to use these power-ups to bring more of what you want into your life. Please note that these are only power-ups—if you don't use them to jump to that platform with the awesome loot, then what good are they?

Chapter 3: Staying Out of the Black hole

If you've ever played video games, you know that they usually have a main goal: defeat the boss and save the world. Let's come up with a made-up game called *Star Crusher*. You pilot a ship, and your goal is to prevent a mysterious race of aliens from destroying every star in the galaxy. Fans of this game have speculated on why these aliens would want to suck the life from the galaxy, and rumors fly about a secret ending that reveals all.

You love the game, and have even uploaded a series of videos online showing off your piloting skills. Lots of people have enjoyed your videos, and you now have a moderate following. In other words, you've had lots of fun playing and entertaining others.

But that secret ending beckons. You want to find it, and envision how much your Internet following could blow up in the coming months if you were to record it and post it online. Many speculate the secret ending is beyond a certain black hole the aliens were first seen around. Getting through it won't be easy—it'll require your ship to be rebuilt with special materials, a strategy to get through the hordes of aliens, and pure luck. So you go to work leveling up your ship's stats, spending hours shooting at smaller enemies to gain points, and using those points to buy better shields, blasters, and bombs. You're putting in hours every day playing *Star Crusher,* despite the boredom of shooting at rogue asteroids and space worms over and over. As the months pass, frustration builds. Your audience gets bored waiting for your secret ending. Some ask you to play a new game while others unsubscribe. You find your blood pressure rising, and soon you're no longer having fun. In fact, you're more miserable than ever.

How did you get into this trap?

The answer can be summed up into one word: want.

Wait, you think. Don't you have to *want* something before you act? And aren't you acting in this situation? What gives?

Yeah, it's confusing. Of course you need to want something before you take action to get it, but there's a difference between *wanting* versus *wanting more.*

When you first started playing *Star Crusher,* you wanted to bring more fun into your life. You did this by, well, having fun and uploading your videos online as a fun experiment. People happened to find your videos and follow you.

Your following grew thanks to your infectious good attitude and your relaxed commentary about blowing up aliens. Unknowingly, you used the Law of Attraction to bring an abundance of fun and relaxation into your life, just by giving those same things to others. You also used several power-ups here to bring more joy into your life—a good attitude, guts (to put yourself out there), ethics (you didn't hack the game or cheat), and your growing knowledge of the game.

But then you *wanted more.* You craved the next big thing—the secret ending—and decided that what you had wasn't good enough. You knew that reaching the secret ending would be long, difficult, and tedious, so you acted accordingly and decided you wouldn't be happy unless you were one of the few players to achieve the new ending. So you began the process you expected, and thus attracted difficulty, boredom, and unhappiness into your life.

In other words, *wanting more* often leads to unhappiness, even in the presence of action. In real life *wanting more* can be compared to the black hole those miserable, star-crushing aliens seemed to emerge from. Some religions even recognize this concept and include it in their teachings. *Wanting more* can only lead to suffering.

Hold it, you think. Does this all mean that if I work hard to achieve my goals, I'll just become miserable? What a raw deal!

Rest assured, that's not what I'm saying. *Wanting more* catches those who act but don't *appreciate* what they have, and everyone who never acts at all. If you let your ship drift through space, just imagining the adventures you could have, the black hole's mighty gravity will eventually pull you in.

You need to act *and* be grateful for what you've attracted. As with actual black holes, recognizing the threat before you find yourself sucked in is the best policy. (Let's talk about the gratitude thing in the next section.)

Wanting More Versus Gratitude

Ah, another "versus." If you've been paying attention, you may have noticed a key difference between your happiness and your misery. When you first started playing *Star Crusher*, it felt good. You had fun playing it, wanted to share it with others, and didn't focus too much on what would happen in the future. You were grateful for the things you had, and maybe even surprised you attracted so many people who enjoyed the videos you made. Maybe you were uncomfortable putting your first videos online, and that's a good thing. Doing something new and worthwhile usually feels like this. (Think of the first time you jumped the ramp on your bike.)

Your fall into misery only started with the decision that you wanted more and put an unrealistic expectation on yourself. You let yourself forget how great you had it before, and as you let your frustration and boredom leak into your videos, you only attracted more misery. Fans left, likes dried up, and your views plummeted. What happened? This doesn't feel good. Things were lining up so well before!

Your comment section devolves into a bunch of trolls. By the time the political arguments show up, you give up and stop taking action. Now you're even more miserable because you let a good thing slip away and can now only dream about becoming an Internet sensation. Or maybe you never even made any *Star Crusher* videos in the first place and it only happened in your mind. By not taking action, or taking the wrong kind of action, you're in a constant state of want. Darkness descends, and feeling helpless, you decide to get a crappy job flipping burgers. You just have to pay the bills, right?

Depressing, isn't it? But realizing this can be a real eye-opener. There is a reason that wealthy people can be miserable and those with far less can be happy. Those who are happy take action *and* are grateful for what they have. They pilot their ships away from the black hole of unhappiness.

I know some people who literally trade in, and obtain, at least two new cars per year, and they're always complaining about something and talking about buying the *Next Big Thing*. Have you ever decided you need the newest gadget on the market, a new television, or a new car to be happy? Now think about how what *wanting more* makes you feel. Perhaps you started working overtime to earn enough money at the expense of sleep, spending time with your family, or taking that long vacation to the Rocky Mountains. Chances are those things don't make you happy. Your *wanting more* (a negative emotion) is only attracting more of the same into your life. You're taking action, but it's the wrong kind. You're trying to force something you think you want into your life instead of enjoying the journey. The same was true in the *Star Crusher* example.

And if you take no action at all? Again, you're always going to be *wanting more.* That doesn't sound like a very fun life to me.

I've experienced all sides of this pyramid, so I can chime in here. I'll start by saying I always wanted to be a writer, but life "got in the way" after high school and I went to college for something that didn't interest me much. By not taking action to bring what I wanted into my life (an abundance of doing what I enjoyed), my college years were a miserable drag with nothing to look forward to because I was in that constant state of want. I felt I could never make writing work as a career. It would never pay, and a publisher would never want what I wrote. I was inside that black hole and unsure how to get out.

Once college drew to a close and I got an "okay" but not very interesting job, I had a bit more free time and decided to give the writing thing a go again. I'd impress agents and force my dream to happen. While this was an improvement over doing nothing, I was still in that black hole. Why? I was too focused on the future; on getting big and finding a publisher. I was also getting overly concerned about delivering what agents wanted instead of enjoying the process of writing and telling stories again. Writing was no longer fun, and I wasn't happy. I still wanted more, and worse, no one wanted my work. I had only dragged more unhappiness into my life.

After a little while, I got sick of the stress and rejection and decided to tell a different story. The first book wasn't working, so maybe I needed to try something different. I got some inspiration from a dream, and my idea felt "right." This time I would relax and enjoy writing the book. I was happier writing this book, a definite improvement over the first, and started hanging out online with other writers. I made friends and joined forums, where I gave back by providing feedback on their work. Most of all, I was having fun writing this new book! Someone even told me about an online contest, and my new book wound up a semifinalist. That was about the time eReaders were getting big, so with this new encouragement, I decided to try a fun experiment. I would upload this book to several eReader stores just to see if anything happened.

Things happened.

And I no longer have to work in that boring job.

Star Crusher, Take Two!

We'll discuss some handy techniques for taking the *right* kind of action to bring great things into your life in the next chapter. But before we do that, let's finish off here on how your *Star Crusher* enterprise could have gone differently had you stopped just dreaming about it and hadn't forced and dragged your way to the Secret Ending.

You've uploaded a video series online about you playing *Star Crusher*. You've heard of the Secret Ending, but after thinking about it, decide you don't want to ruin the fun you're having. So you tell your followers you'll keep playing, exploring new aspects of the game, and maybe find a few surprises on the way. Who knows what could happen?

Since you're having fun, you continue to attract more followers, and one of them is a fellow gamer—a *popular* gamer—who also makes videos. He thinks you have talent, likes your attitude, and wants you to join him in making *Star Crusher* videos. It's a scary thought, but it feels "right", and you know it'll be fun. Unable to believe how well things are lining up, you say yes. It almost seems like the universe is working *for* you! It's almost as if your happiness and gratitude are attracting more of the same.

Things explode. The two of you work together and are able to make the preparations you need to reach the Secret Ending with far less stress, and it's more fun now that you have a gaming buddy. In a couple months, you and your new friend charge the black hole, get through, and discover the aliens' plot to destroy all light because they're attracted to, and feed on, misery. But they're no match for you, and the two of you are the first to achieve the Secret Ending!

Chapter 4: Crushing It
Five Powerful Techniques To Help Steer Your Ship

As you read in the last chapter, to bring an abundance of great things into your life, it's necessary to, one, take action, and two, take the right kind of action. Both are necessary to keep your ship away from destruction. First, you need to steer your ship, and second, you must steer your ship in the right direction to avoid your enemies and keep from getting sucked into the black hole.

So how do you do that? You'll need knowledge of how your ship handles, the guts to get in the pilot's chair, a good attitude (the belief you can do this), and brainpower. Health may help your reaction time, while not ejecting from the ship and leaving your crewmates to certain death is also a major plus. (You don't want them surviving and coming back to kill you, do you?)

Of course, you're still playing *Star Crusher*. Imagine you're with your famous gaming partner, you're recording this for the world to see, and you're about to go for that Secret Ending. You've already prepared your ship by upgrading it. After months of practice, this is the moment. So what techniques can you employ to max out your chances of achieving the end that you want, and, by extension, attracting more of what you want into your life?

You need a strategy.

What, you were going to leave navigating through this black hole up to luck after everything's lined up so well for you? You were just going to dive in before millions of people and probably end up humiliating yourself, losing your awesome ship, and having to start over?

Of course not! If you're using your knowledge power-up here, you'll likely have studied the game mechanics of *Star Crusher* to learn how your enemies behave, what their weaknesses are, and what happens in the space around a black hole. Then you and your gaming partner have sat down with one another and come up with a plan. First, you'll need to get through the debris field that surrounds the black hole, and since you've both had experience flying through asteroid fields, you decide the best way to do so is to have one of you use your Triple Blaster. You also now know the aliens around the black hole will try to fight you with floating mines, and come up with a strategy to eliminate these, too. And after doing some research on your new weapons, as well as on some crazy science, you know the Wormhole Gun *might* open a portal to another dimension if you fire it at the black hole itself. (This last one is a risk and a theory, but remember, no one else has figured out how to get to the Secret Ending before.)

Have a buddy, or buddies, to keep you on your toes.

Looks like you have this covered already. With two of you working together toward a common goal, you can encourage and watch out for each other during the final battle. Maybe you've reminded each other to log into *Star Crusher* for daily gaming sessions and prevented the other from slacking off, even if it's only for thirty minutes per day. (Remember—you still likely have a day job at this point or other responsibilities, and you're tired at the end of the day. Your gaming buddy makes you put in some practice even on days where you don't feel like logging on.)

A real-life area where a buddy system is important is losing weight or getting healthier. You've probably seen diet advice that involves having a friend diet with you, or having a family member help keep track of what you're eating and how much exercise you're putting in per week. Other people can do wonders to keep you accountable (and moving!) in other areas of your life, too.

Aside: When I was just getting serious about my writing and striving to get published, I joined a group of writers online who expected me to post new material often to have it critiqued. This forced me to keep writing, even on days where I didn't feel like sitting down at the keyboard. I can only imagine I helped my new buddies do the same, too.

Today, I have others help keep me accountable by consistently announcing my release dates on new material. I also attend a real-life local critique group, and it works! Just the desire not to let my readers down is what makes me sit at the keyboard every day and make that deadline.

Stop telling yourself you can't.

I admit, I still struggle with this one on some days, and I imagine you do, too. I've published and sold material for years, and there are certainly days where I feel like it's too much and I can't do everything I need to do.

This is where you need to reach inside and pull out that good attitude. You can find one, right? If you can't find that happy place hiding under all those rain clouds, simply saying to yourself, "I can do this," or, "I can stick to my healthy eating," can help. Just make sure you avoid negative statements like, "I will not eat that cake," or, "I won't fail this test." Remember that like attracts like, and negative statements will attract negative statements into your life. Your subconscious doesn't like "no," or, "not," or, "won't," and might even turn the meaning around on you! "I will fail this test," isn't what you're going for.

Say your positive statements over and over if you have to. Eventually, your subconscious mind will pick up the message, and you might find yourself more willing to take the previously "impossible" action. Of course, this doesn't substitute for action, but you need to grab onto that mindset first.

Remember when you first heard about the Secret Ending? You thought, "It will take forever and be very hard to reach it." Or you thought, "I might not have enough time," or, "I'm too busy." I hear that last one from dissatisfied people a lot, though it's rarely true. Even carving out a few minutes a day to reach your goals is far better than nothing! Progress is progress—it *will* snowball.

And yet, when you changed your mindset and decided to have fun, to do what felt "right", you unconsciously changed your tune to, "Maybe this can happen." You were no longer focused on how hard it would be to reach the Secret Ending or on the fact that no one had ever reached it before. Instead, you simply acted, and now the Secret Ending is right in front of you.

Look for what others have done.

You probably learned a lot from your new gaming buddy in a much shorter amount of time than you would have playing *Star Crusher* alone. Chances are before you even started playing, you checked out some videos of others playing *Star Crusher* and learned how to progress through the beginning levels of the game. You probably also learned how *not* to play *Star Crusher.* You watched that guy crash his ship when he failed to do maintenance on his engine to save a few credits. That video with the other guy piloting his ship into an asteroid belt without a shield also didn't go over so well, did it?

You took these ideas with you when you began playing, which gave you a leg up over other new players. That knowledge power-up sure came in handy, didn't it? Later, when you paired up with your new gaming buddy, the two of you continued to see how more advanced players navigated the game, and forums proved to hold a wealth of information.

This point is true whether you're playing a video game, losing weight, or even finding The One. Look at how many books exist on how to attract the love of your life, how to make more money, and how to improve your health. Furthermore, look at who's usually giving out this advice: those who have already attracted an abundance of wealth, happiness, or love. (Provided they're ethical and not lying, of course.)

When looking for diet advice, you're not going to listen to some guy with a beer gut. You won't buy a book about relationships from someone who's been married and divorced a dozen times. You'll look for people who have achieved what you want, and you'll see what they did to get where they are. Best of all, you'll know that the advice they offer can *work.*

Chip Away A Little At A Time.

When you first find the knowledge you'll need to succeed in any endeavor, the advice probably sounds overwhelming. This is normal, and is no cause for alarm. Perhaps you had a mini stroke when you heard about how difficult it would be, and how much work it would take, to reach *Star Crusher's* secret ending. You'd have to level up your ship, complete numerous mini quests, gather millions of credits, research which equipment you'll need, study the game's mechanics, and more. If that sounds like a lot, it is. Many people give up at this step and stop taking action.

But there's a way to get through that, too. The trick is to chip away at it a little at a time.

Having another person get involved certainly helps. What you want to do here is turn a huge task into a bunch of smaller, more manageable tasks.

Perhaps one day you focus on one side quest in *Star Crusher* and rescue a science team from the aliens who then award you several thousand credits. Maybe the next night you're a bit more tired, so you browse the Star Crusher forums and read a few posts on some secret planets you can visit, discovering a secret base where you can buy the Wormhole Gun. The next day you just play aimlessly, taking out an alien fleet and earning some experience points—points you'll need to be able to use the Wormhole Gun. And so on, and so on. Instead of focusing on how overwhelming your journey is, you take things one step at a time, and in a couple of months, you find you're halfway to your goal!

Of course, how quickly you can reach your goal will depend on a lot of things. You may be able to only focus on one or two things per day that will get you closer to your goal, or you may be able to focus on five or six smaller things. Either way, you will be making progress.

Take my occupation. There's a *lot* to do. Not only must I write, but I must also manage advertising, edit, decide what I want my covers to look like, send out newsletters, write blurbs, study the market, interact with other authors, upload manuscripts, format, and more. If I were to stare down all these tasks at once, there would be a hole in my wall from me banging my head so much.

Small tasks are a lifesaver and keep me going. I write, working on a couple of different projects, and then play with some advertising for a few minutes. The next day I'll write again and explore some cover concepts, but it gets done, and that's what matters. When I just started out on my writing journey, I'd do a couple of things per day to bring me closer to my goal (turning my writing into my only career). Back then, I tackled things one at a time and paced myself. Starting out by writing, say, a thousand words a day and setting up one ad got me used to the bigger stuff that came later.

Now that I've made more progress in my writing career, I've upped the ante to doing a few things per day to bring more wealth and happiness into my life.

Of course, these tactics aren't the whole story or the only thing you need to look at to take effective action in your life and get the universe to work for you. If you're still playing *Star Crusher*, you know there are more traps than first meets the eye, and on the next page we'll go after a particularly nasty set of real-life traps: bad habits. Like a police officer who hides off the road in order to catch unsuspecting speeders, bad habits can bring your success journey to a halt. Time to learn how to avoid the traffic stop and the resulting ticket.

Chapter 5: Knock It Off! Avoiding the Debuffs

Okay, I'm using another term most often seen in video games. If you're familiar with gaming, you'll know what a debuff is. It's actually a pretty common term, found throughout many types of games, but as with fantasy worlds, there are real-life debuffs, too.

A debuff is basically anything that slows you down or slows your progress. In a video game, your character could obtain, say, a Slowness debuff, which (predictably) makes you run at a snail's pace. In real life, you might contract the flu, which would slow you down for a week or so. When you're navigating the game of life, there are just as many debuffs lurking out there as there are power-ups. In this chapter, we'll go over the more common debuffs just waiting to block your abundance or even stop your progress. (We can also call these things bad habits, but that's kind of boring, isn't it?)

So what debuffs can you expect to meet (and avoid) in your abundance journey? We'll focus more on the ones that you create rather than on external debuffs such as accidents or getting fired from your job. These are the roadblocks you can do something about. Uplifting thought, isn't it?

Debuff #1: Excuses, excuses.

We touched on this in the last chapter a bit. When you use excuses to avoid going after your dream, you do nothing but slam the door on any abundance that might have been waiting to come your way. Let's look at a hypothetical woman named Michelle. Michelle has a dream of traveling to exotic locales and has always wanted to visit Alaska. Maybe she wants to go on one of those cruises and whale watch. Believing she can go on her trip would give Michelle a higher chance of actually taking her dream vacation, but instead, Michelle focuses on why she can't go.

"I work sixty hours a week at the office."

"It would be too expensive. I could never afford a cruise."

"What would my coworkers do while I'm gone? The office wouldn't run without me."

You can see what Michelle's doing. By telling herself these things, she's making sure she will never get to leave her boring box and see the world. She's keeping her world small and attracting more boredom, and as we know, most offices aren't very fun places to work. There are no whales there.

Michelle might also say, "Well, I can save the money, and once I retire in thirty years, I'll go on my trip."

This last excuse is a particularly dangerous one. Michelle may feel like she's doing something to reach her goal, but all she's doing is postponing her trip with another excuse. Not only is she attracting more of the same-ol' into her life (boring job, lack of fun), she's setting herself up for very possible disappointment.

Aside: I used to work in health care. During that time, I met many people who were retired. Not to get depressing, but a good portion of those retirees weren't out living their dreams or taking vacations. They were going to appointment after appointment for their back pain, fighting numerous health problems, keeping track of meds, and the like. Some couldn't even tolerate sitting in the car for more than thirty minutes at a time, let alone a plane. Most commonly, these folks had to sit down after walking for a few minutes at a time. Not very conducive to a cruise, is it?

If Michelle tells herself that *now* is the time to plan that trip, no excuses, she's much more likely to go and catch some amazing shots of whales leaping out of the ocean. Why? Believing it's possible will propel Michelle to cut some unnecessary spending, skip the Starbucks, and quickly save enough money to book that cruise. She'll find a way.

Debuff #2: Letting Yourself Go.

Lousy health, as I mentioned in the aside above, will chase away any abundance of happiness, friends, or success in no time. Bad health attracts sadness, frustration, boredom, and maybe even poverty if you live in an area where medical bills can pile up.

Take care of yourself. You'll feel much better and more energetic if you eat fruits, vegetables, and natural proteins versus pizza, soda, and other junk food. You'll feel more alive if you get up and move around, even if you just take a walk around the block. Getting enough sleep will clear your mind and improve your mood like you wouldn't believe.

Is it easy? Heck no, but tell yourself that it's possible and well worth it. Don't fall on any excuses, because *bad health can ruin everything.* (In the next chapter, I'll go over how I kicked this debuff, along with many of these others, to the curb.)

Debuff #3: Expecting Your Ship To Explode.

Let's imagine you're piloting the spacecraft from the last couple of chapters and you're about to dive into an asteroid field. When you see the enormous field in front of you, do you think, "Now's the time to test my skills," or do you think, "I'm so going to die here and humiliate myself?"

Which mindset do you think is more likely to get you through the asteroid field?

If you guessed, "I'm so going to die here," then you need to work on breaking this bad habit. This is the same as telling yourself that you can't handle a promotion to a better position or you can't attract your true love. With this mindset, how can you ever *want* to take action and claim the life you want?

If all you can imagine is a disastrous future, that's what you will get. You won't try too hard to steer your ship through the asteroids, and yes, you'll crash into one and embarrass yourself just as you predicted. Enjoy your self-fulfilling prophecy.

Debuff #4: Telling Yourself You Suck.

We've all done it—told ourselves we're terrible at math, or putting things together, or getting a date, or even at sports. A child who believes he's terrible at basketball will never get on the court and practice. A woman who believes she's unattractive will act accordingly and never find the person of her dreams—or worse, she'll attract a terrible mate who leaves their underwear on the living room floor and walks out one day for another person. Everyone has a Negative Nelly inside them who delights in calling you an idiot for picking up that scam phone call or hitting the curb with your car.

It's time to start high-fiving Negative Nelly in the face. With a chair. Imagine yourself doing it if necessary. This nasty inner voice serves no purpose other than to keep you in your safe box for your entire life. Well, usually. If Negative Nelly says you'll get eaten if you dive into shark-infested waters, and that it's a stupid idea to do so, you should probably listen. That's just common sense.

Debuff #5: Want, Want, Want!

Yeah, we went over this already. Wanting more is a major debuff in itself, and forces your attention away from what you already have. When you instead focus on what you've already attracted, be it money, love, creativity, or even friends, you're more encouraged to get out there and grab more! Wanting just makes you focus on what you don't have. Focusing on the vacuum in your life will attract more of the same. Not seeing the love your partner is giving you already will probably entice them to leave. Feeling like you can't finish that painting won't inspire you to paint another, and feeling like your life can only ever be dull will keep you in that office cube.

Debuff #6: Relying On Everyone and Everything Else To Make You Happy.

Big mistake. You are responsible for your own happiness. I'll repeat that. No one except *you* can give you the life you want. Not your partner, not your friends, and not your child. Sure, they can help, but the decision is ultimately up to you.

Imagine a woman, Trina, who hates being alone so much that she's told herself she can't be happy without a man in her life. See what Trina's doing? She's placing her happiness on another person. When she gets a boyfriend, Neal, she becomes overly clingy, believing only he can bring satisfaction to her life. By placing her own power (and responsibility) on Neal, Trina may feel happy for a short time before Neal realizes she's draining his energy and sanity. Neal begins to feel responsible for her and starts believing it's his job to, say, stop her from stress drinking. It's not fair to him. As he struggles more and more to maintain Trina's happiness, he pulls away to protect himself. The two break up, and Trina finds herself single again.

Trina dates again soon after, and this time she attracts a man, Paul, who discovers he can use her weakness to his benefit. Trina gives him her power in exchange for her happiness, and Paul becomes possessive and controlling. Trina, not wanting to be single, ends up in a bad marriage. Neal was a good boyfriend, but by not taking responsibility for her own happiness, she chased him away.

Debuff #7: Distraction!

Put down your smartphone. Get off Facebook. Get stuff done. Being able to pull away from common distractions will supercharge your goals, whether it's to spend more time with your family or chase a new career.

How many times a day have you found yourself wanting to check your notifications? Perhaps you get online for just a minute and find yourself reading some shocking news story. Then you scroll down to the comments section and follow every argument that pops up. There's the political argument. The racist jerk. The troll. Despite this being a story about puppies, the whole roster has showed up and it's mesmerizing.

An hour passes. You click on another link, and then another hour disappears. You look up, and it's dinner time! That test you were supposed to study for happens tomorrow.

Social media is fun and useful, but it can quickly become an addictive time suck. It can be a powerful tool in your journey or a major stumbling block. The key is to block out the distractions. Maybe you have to unfollow some people, cut down on your notifications, and close your account on some sites to focus on bringing an abundance of real things into your life.

Debuff #8: Feeling Like A Jerkwad.

If you're thinking of moving to another part of the country to take a new job, you may feel bad about leaving your family behind or abandoning your friends. So you pass on the offer and keep slaving away in your cube. If you're on a diet, you might feel terrible about passing on that fry platter your friends have just ordered, so you dig in to fit in. Hello weight gain.

Or maybe you regret something you did in the past, like not showing up to your best friend's birthday party. As a result, you feel so bad you stop going to your friends' parties, because jerks don't deserve to, right?

This is a hard debuff to overcome. Moving away from family or forgiving our past mistakes is hard. It's difficult, but not impossible. Don't set yourself on fire to make others warm. Besides, if your friends and family are real and not just trying to manipulate you, they'll support what brings you more happiness so long as you're not stealing from or murdering anybody, right?

In the next chapter, I'll discuss my personal journey into better health and talk about how these debuffs held me back for decades. More importantly, I'll tell you how I managed to overcome them. And a bit later, we'll go into some weapons you can use to fight off these bad habits and gain the life you want!

Chapter 6: Real Life, Real Example

When I'm trying to learn a new concept or technique, whether it's a new mode of thinking or a new strategy to make more money (yes, we'll get to money in a later chapter), I always like to see examples of how things work. That's why your math teacher always solved problems on the board and why successful entrepreneurs like sharing success stories. Examples are awesome, and make understanding things so much easier.

Since lots of people have the goal of losing weight or getting healthier, I figured it would be great to include my own personal example. First, I'll go over the depressing stuff, the debuffs that held me back for years. Then I'll get to the more uplifting stuff, discussing the power-ups I used and the mindset I adopted to get myself out of the bad-health rut I had fallen into. (I'll refer back to the earlier chapters throughout my story.)

Frequent headaches, fatigue, muscle aches, and creeping weight gain made up my reality for years of my life, starting when I graduated high school. An abundance of health is something I didn't have, and as the years passed, things weren't getting any better. My blood pressure also slowly started to creep up, and sleep deprivation with a topping of job and commute-related stress weren't helping matters, either. When I was still in my health care job, I would leave my house early in the morning and get home at close to seven PM, leaving me with the task of figuring out dinner when I got home. I'd often fall back on something I could just throw in the microwave or order from a drive-thru, and as we all know, those kinds of foods tend to not be very healthy for you. And since I'm a night person, rising early took its own toll, forcing me to turn to energy drinks at times just to stay awake.

I didn't want to be a hypocrite with too much weight and not enough health, especially since I worked in an occupation that involved getting people up and moving again. So, I started making efforts to lose weight and improve my health.

But I started out the wrong way and unconsciously applied debuffs to myself. First, I had let myself go in the first place (Debuff #2 from the last chapter). Headaches were near daily at this point, and my weight was getting up to a level that would have been embarrassing had I gone for a checkup. Not feeling good sure sucked the enjoyment out of the free time I did have, and at one point, I had severe heartburn for almost a month that took a bunch of meds to get rid of. My stomach never really felt all that good in general, and mood swings were another layer on the cake of unhappiness.

Once I got sick of feeling sick, I made my first attempts to get healthier. Though I was taking action, I still had several debuffs standing in the way of bringing more health to myself.

The next problem? I was depending on others to bring me health—namely mainstream health advice sanctioned by well-meaning governments (and, as I found out later, major food companies). I did things "right" and ate lots of grains, including whole grains, and stuck to skim milk and other low-fat products. I also cut the amount I was eating and made sure to take walks every day. While exercising certainly helped some, and still benefits me, I found that the recommended diet left me tired, cranky, and craving more. I couldn't stick to my new diet for more than a week or two at a time.

I tried multiple times to "do it right", but always to the same results, and my weight kept creeping upward. So, eventually I told myself that I sucked at this and that it was too hard to get healthy in today's society. (See two more debuffs there?) My time spent working in health care had also given me the belief that everyone feels lousy all the time, especially as they get older, and that bad health was inevitable as we age. I expected my ship to explode.

Now, how did I get out of this mess?

To make a long story short, I realized my life was in danger. I won't go over what exactly happened to make me realize this, but trust me, there's nothing like a good old-fashioned wake-up call to flip a switch in your brain. I needed to change my reality, and *I needed to do it now.*

While exploring ways to lose weight and improve my health, I had come across some articles online about cutting grains (and sugar) and had read some testimonials from people who had lost a lot of weight and felt better. At the time, I dismissed it as a fad diet, or a fringe idea, or simply too hard to do. How could I cut all bread, pasta, cereal, sandwiches, etc. from my diet? Sugar was understandable, but grains? They're in everything! It was already hard enough to cook one meal a day. Besides, mainstream advice said you needed grains to be healthy, and of course to avoid fat.

But then I looked at my results by following mainstream advice. Since government-sanctioned, mainstream diet advice had done great things for our health and waistlines (sarcasm), then maybe it was time to try something different. Maybe those fringe people were onto something.

I had to learn more. I did some online research and discovered maybe I didn't know everything about nutrition. I decided to try this no-grain, no sugar thing. The idea was scary, since the habit change involved eating more fat, but I'd see what happened. It seemed to work well for others who struggled the way I did.

The first few days were brutal. I went from having easy sandwiches and cereal to eating eggs, nuts, boiled veggies, salads (no croutons!), some meat, some fruit, fish, cheese, etc. I had to make grain-free lunches to take to work since finding food I could eat was nearly impossible at the neighboring Subway. I spent more time in the kitchen, but worst of all, I had body aches and headaches for those first days. My body was in withdrawal. Going to the grocery store was torture. I was tempted with a dozen aisles of things I couldn't have. Grains? Out. Added sugar? Nope, and that turned out to be in every low-fat, "healthy" product ever. I couldn't even buy a bottle of ketchup! I found myself limited to the outer ring of the grocery store. I had to skip everything in the middle except for the frozen veggies.

But instead of telling myself it was too hard, that I sucked, or that it would take too long for me to start feeling better, I told myself I could do it, that I *had* to do it. Things were different now. During that first grocery shopping trip, I thought, *maybe I can pick up a box of candy.* But then I told myself to *GET OUT*, and I bought my things and got the heck out of the store.

I could have focused on how hard this all was, and on how I might have to do this for the rest of my life, but decided to focus instead on the possibility that I could feel great and have a normal lifespan instead. Those are no small rewards. Focusing on the positive kept me going—I would take this one day at a time.

Nothing much changed at first, but I decided to be patient and see what happened. I had lost a couple of pounds during the first week, but instead of bemoaning that I hadn't lost more, I felt grateful I had done that and kept going. The withdrawal headaches vanished. So did the muscle aches. Since I was still eating some meat and cheese, I felt full after my meals and not crabby, as I had before. Best of all, I had energy and wanted to exercise, and my cravings for grains and sugar faded.

Then, two weeks into my new eating habits, my pants fell down.

Thankfully, I was standing in my kitchen and not in public. Usually your pants falling down is a bad thing, but not in this case. This was working! I wanted to stick my middle finger up to all the advice I'd been given since elementary school that never worked.

Aside: Do you notice the power-ups I was using here? Combined with action, my new knowledge, patience, positive attitude, and guts (which I needed to try something so drastic) were bringing me results. I also changed my mental traits, telling myself this change was good. I needed to realize that good health was out there for me to steal. Most of all, I was willing to see that my old attempts weren't working and that wasn't going to change. I took action.

Now, this lifestyle change wasn't without its snags. Eating out is hard. Going to parties is hard. Sometimes I don't want to cook. I still have to avoid the entire middle section of the grocery store (though I can have dark chocolate and sometimes even limited-ingredient vanilla ice cream). Focusing on what I had already gained from this (or lost, I should say) helped me stay on track because it was encouraging.

The Five Powerful Techniques helped me to steer my ship. I employed all of them to keep myself out of the black hole. First, others gave me encouragement when I told them what I was trying. Coworkers would come up to me and remark on how I'd lost weight, even before I noticed in the mirror! I had already set my strategy (no grains or sugar, no exceptions) and stopped telling myself I couldn't do it. I looked at what others had done.

As for chipping away a bit at a time, I employed that, too, but later. After I had lost my first twenty pounds, I hit a plateau and stopped losing. So, after more research, I decided to stop eating industrial oils, too, (such as soybean and canola oil). That meant throwing out potato chips and a few other processed foods I was still eating. Consequently, I started losing weight again. In other words, I didn't throw out everything unhealthy all at once, but did it a few items at a time.

So, where am I today? What's my reality?

My weight is down to normal and has stayed there for over two years. My sinuses cleared up. I have more energy and don't feel sleepy after meals (unless I eat something I'm not supposed to). Headaches are much rarer, and so are muscle aches. Last time I checked my blood pressure, it was 106/77 (optimal) when it was borderline high before. My skin is softer, heartburn is almost nonexistent, and best of all, my mind has cleared. This last one has had a great effect on my writing! Reviews on my books got better, and I started to sell more.

I'd also like to add that at the same time in my life, the mindset changes and the power-ups I learned helped me to break out of my day job and make writing my only career. My better health and attitude enabled me to put in the work necessary to change my work life for the better, too! My happiness with my improved health only brought more happiness into my life, and I can't wait to see this effect continue to snowball.

In the next chapter, we'll talk about some good habits you can adopt to further help you on your journey, whatever it may be. And in the chapter after that, we'll talk about everyone's favorite subject, the abundance of money!

Chapter 7: Five Awesome Weapons For Success

Okay, we're about to talk about video games again, because those are fun and hold our attention better than some boring office meeting where your manager talks about goals and projections. Who wants to read a chapter riddled with eyeroll-worthy office jargon? I'm not going to tell you to "get your ducks in a row" or to "get the ball rolling". If you want to find more of these jargon phrases, type "annoying office jargon" into your search engine. Bingo!

So, I'm going to compare these great habits you can work on to the weapons you can outfit your spaceship with. That's a lot more exciting, right? If you've played any type of action game, whether it be a war game, a platformer, or even one where you're piloting your spaceship, you'll know that obtaining the right weapons is the key to success. Like power ups, the right blasters, shields, and floating space mines can help you beat the game.

In this chapter, I'll go over the amazing weapons you can use to blast your way to the loot you're seeking. Equip your ship with them, and you'll soon find you're going places.

(You might want to get a notebook for some of these habits, as writing might help make everything more tangible and concrete. Or maybe I'm saying this because I'm a writer. A computer will work just as well for keeping things organized!)

What are you thinking and saying?

Take some time today to listen to your thoughts. Your brain is chattering all the time, to the point where it's all background noise. Think of your conscious mind as a big message board, complete with ever-changing post-it notes and reminders. Maybe, if you wanted to keep to the gaming example, it could be the chat that appears in the bottom corner of your screen.

Not only do you see the constant, rolling chat in your display (known as your thoughts), but your subconscious also reads these. And, if you've been paying attention, you know your subconscious mind can help drive your actions in the background, positive or negative, sometimes without you knowing why.

Sometimes you use voice chat, too. Your words are just as powerful as your thoughts— perhaps even more so. What kinds of things are you saying to others (or even to yourself) as you play? Your subconscious listens to your words, too, and not just your thoughts.

If you're hitting a snag bringing what you want into your life, it's worth pausing your game for a moment so you can watch the chat.

What kinds of messages are you telling yourself?

Are you telling yourself this game sucks, the design is bad, and the bugs make it unplayable? Or are you telling yourself that despite a few bugs, you can get around them and still have fun? Are you saying you can exploit a certain bug to get farther in the game and try out a mechanic no one else has attempted before?

If you tell yourself the game sucks and isn't fair, what action will you take? You'll likely turn off the game and give up. After all, a defective space mine that doesn't blow up anything metal (such as the alien ships) isn't very useful. Or is it?

Tell yourself the bug might get you somewhere, and you'll feel inclined to investigate instead of quitting. You know asteroids can contain metals, and the bombs can still blow up rocks, so you discover an easy way to space mine and gather materials. Hello riches!

So, take a few minutes today and watch your thoughts as they enter your mind. Write some of them down. Many will be about your daily life and some will even be about things you plan to do today. What are you thinking?

What do you need to change?

See the big universe.

Okay, so the universe is big. Just a few minutes' worth of reading about it will tell you that. If the programmers of your spaceship game are any good, they've taken this into account as well. There are many planets and stars to explore.

Many people can't see a world beyond their daily lives. Maybe they know it's out there, that there are multiple countries, cultures, occupations, and experiences they can choose from, but some never get past their daily commute to work and their same routine. Some never force themselves to see something new. This could be a new job, a public park in another city, a location across the country, or even a new date. These people focus only on a narrow reality. Perhaps they're so immersed in their current job they never have time to go anywhere else. Maybe they focus so much on a partner that broke up with them that they never want to meet anyone else.

So, what weapon can you use to get out of this rut?

Simply sit down for a few minutes each day and try to see the bigger universe, even if it's only in your mind. Write these ideas down if that helps. Imagine yourself dating a new person or going to a new gym. Maybe imagine a trip to somewhere you've never been before. Just opening your mind up to the greater world of possibility will set you up to actually get there.

Give thanks daily.

What do you have so far? What thing in your life is making you happy today?

Get out your notebook or open your computer file. Every day, write down one thing you're thankful for. It can be a supportive family, a paycheck, or even the fact that you're breathing air. Write down something, anything. Focusing on the positive will help put you in the mindset to bring more great stuff into your life. Remember the subconscious?

If you don't want to write it down, simply reflecting will work as well. Maybe you can do this as you're falling asleep or waking up in the morning.

I certainly have more energy to get work done in my writing career when I feel like things are going right and I can focus on the positive stuff that's happening. Think of the last time you had great stuff going on. Maybe you just had a great first date with someone, and as you reflect on it, you're more likely to pick up the phone and ask that person on a second date. If you just got a promotion or raise at work, you're more likely to put in the effort to go even farther if you focus on what you've accomplished so far.

Sharing Is Caring.

Unless you're skipping around this book, you'll have read examples of people sharing their success with others. Remember the weight loss blog I mentioned? This habit is similar. Sharing what you're passionate about, especially to those who could benefit from your passion, is a great way to give yourself confidence in your chosen area.

Let's say you enjoy long-distance running. Maybe you create a blog about fitness to help those who want to improve their health and stamina. Not only do you feel good about yourself, you feel good about the people you're helping. At the same time, you're building your online identity and bringing more of what you want to yourself (in this case, encouragement and happiness that you're helping others). Maybe you start a running blog and post a short story about a run down a nature trail and another about eating habits that help you perform at your best. By sharing, you attract online friends, connections, and a growing following. And if you want to write a book about running, what do you think will happen? You already have fans waiting to snap it up!

This same habit worked well for you when you made your videos about playing *Star Crusher*. You shared regularly and attracted a following as a result, and you did this without realizing what you were doing at first!

This weapon is also vital when it comes to making more money. Building an online following is often necessary to run a business, or even to sell the crafts you've made in your kitchen. Even a page on social media is better than nothing. Share, share, share regularly, and you will attract those who share your interest or need your services. We live in the Internet age where sharing is easier than ever.

Personally, I have a newsletter and run a couple of social media groups to spread the word about my writing. I share regularly (about 2-3 times per month) and include stories related to my progress. Over the years, I've attracted people interested in the types of stories I tell, and it has done nothing but bring me an abundance of what I want—to get my stories out there.

Become a Guru.

Wouldn't it be nice if you could wave a wand and become a master at something in an instant? Unfortunately, the universe doesn't work that way, but before you feel cheated, take a moment and think about one of the Five Powerful Techniques I talked about earlier: chipping away a little at a time.

Chipping away at something a little at a time can lead to huge results, and now's your chance. What I want you to do is give yourself a goal. Right now. I don't care if it's to go on that cruise or to open a business selling rhinoceros repellent. (Seriously, those things are dangerous!) The point is to set a goal, chip away a little at a time, and prove to yourself that you can do it. By extension, you'll also prove to yourself that you can become the master of your reality.

Write down your goal. Now write down a list of things you'll have to do to get there. (Some research might be necessary here.) If you're opening a business, your list might include saving money, deciding on a demographic, figuring out the taxes, getting a product ready, lining up your marketing, etc. That's a lot, to say the least, but with your list in hand, you can start chipping away a little at a time. Unless you're a deity, you won't accomplish all these things at once (and maybe not even then!).

Do one or two of these things a day. There are 365 days per year, and if you keep in the habit of chipping away, you'll have a fantastic grip on your rhinoceros repellent in no time.

Perhaps you begin with simple research. You figure out that selling it to safari tourists (your demographic) is the way to go. After a few days of reading safari stories, you realize there's a demand for rhino repellent. Rhinos are scary. Great! The next day, you research what smells rhinos hate. The next day, you figure out what chemicals make those smells. The next day, you speak with a chemist on how to make your spray. A couple of months in, you look up how to register your business. Then you figure out all the tax stuff the month after that. Perhaps on another day, you purchase your website domain, and on another day, you join a safari forum. On a day after that, you start sharing your own safari stories on the forum, including some scary ones with charging rhinos. You make friends and gain a following over the next several weeks.

See how much progress you're making by focusing on one small thing per day? That's a lot more digestible than trying to put it all together at once. You've identified your product, the need for it, what will make it work, and who you're selling it to. You're also building your following. You've got a product in the works and your website is coming together. You could say that by the end of that year, you're a guru on rhino repellent, and it didn't even take that much work. Best of all, you've proven to yourself what you're capable of!

Of course, you don't *have* to make rhino repellent. Making a list and sticking to it is a great way to reach any goal.

Just so I don't overwhelm you, I'll end the chapter here so you can start using these five weapons. Start today. No excuses, remember?

In the next chapter, we'll go over a few more great habits to bring you the life you want. Then we'll start talking about money. Promise! But don't skip these calls to action. They'll make all the difference between success and failure.

Chapter 8: Completing Your Arsenal
A Few More Weapons To Fight Back Against Failure

Yeah, I know. That's a long chapter title, but I had trouble thinking of something shorter.

In the last chapter, we talked about five weapons you can use to fight that monster that's always lurking right behind you: failure and unhappiness. (Okay, so that's two monsters.) As with any monster, you want to have plenty of options, right? If I'm facing a rhino that can trample me at any moment, to be honest, I'll want something more than rhino repellent spray. There's always the chance the rhino has a cold and can't smell, or that it will dodge my aim and cause me to have a very bad day. Maybe I'm not a very good shot with the spray, so I'll want to have a couple of other options as well. A vehicle I can use to escape is probably the best option, and one I think most people would take before using that little spray bottle.

I'm not saying that carrying rhino repellent spray is a bad idea. I'm saying that not everyone benefits from the same thing, so it's always good to have other options. Some of the techniques in these two chapters will work well for some, while others might not benefit as much and will need to use some other weapons.

Look at movies. A ninja will do better against his enemy by choosing throwing stars, while a soldier will do best with a sniper rifle, and an archer will no doubt go with a bow. Real life is the same. The trick is to find a few techniques that work well for you. Try all these techniques and see which ones bring you the best results. That's part of the fun, right?

From the last chapter, I've found benefits in using all the weapons. Personally, I do the best by sharing my progress regularly with my newsletter and by breaking up my tasks so I'm not overwhelmed every day. When I get up each morning, I pick a few tasks to focus on that day, even if I have far more than that to take care of.

I've also had good success with looking at all the great possibilities and trying new things. There are so many genres to try writing!

But let's discuss a few more great weapons you can use to attract what you want into your life.

Look at what you've done!
No, I don't mean this in a bad way. When you hear this phrase, it usually has a negative vibe, so let's go with, *look at what you've accomplished so*

far. The word "accomplished" is a lot more positive, and if you've been paying attention, you'll know that your mind likes those positive words. No more negativity for you!

(Correction: Loads of good things for you!)

This weapon is a lot like having gratitude, but not quite. When you look at what you've accomplished so far, you're looking at, well, that. If you have the goal of making rhino repellent, you've accomplished something by just researching the idea. Sadly, many people never get past the dreaming stage of their goals and never take that first action to change their lives and grab that abundance waiting for them.

A perfect example of this would come from when I was still at my old job, years ago. Many of my coworkers knew I was a writer. A few came up to me and said, "I've always dreamed of being a writer!"

You can probably see where this is going. The people saying this phrase had never even tried to write the first page of a book. They only dreamed about it, and probably told themselves they were too busy/not talented enough to try writing a book. They were finished before they even started.

But I had already started, and I realized I had accomplished what others had not: I had taken that first action. Maybe I wasn't the best writer years ago, but this thought bolstered me and made me realize I'd gotten over a hurdle that many never pass. I practiced. I accomplished more, and more, and more. Simply looking back at what I'd already checked off my list told me what I needed—that if I had already written, I could write more.

I want you to get out your notebook (or computer file, or journal) and write down what you've already accomplished to bring more abundance into your life. I don't care if all you've done is make a dating profile online, or if you've written the first page of a book, or if you've even looked up diets online. The point is, you've taken action. Write it down. One thing is going the way you want!

Feel better and more confident? Good! Now you'll be a lot more likely to accomplish something else on your journey, and soon you'll find your list growing.

And if you haven't taken that first step? Do it now. Write that first page. Make that dating profile. Sign up for that class you've wanted to take. Then write it down in your journal. See how easy that was?

Tomorrow, add to that list. Do something else that helps attract what you want, even if it's small. Look at that list as it grows and pat yourself on the back.

(This weapon is best used with the *Becoming A Guru* one, if you haven't noticed.)

Find the hacks that others have used to grow.

You've probably heard about "life hacks". You've likely seen the videos on how to make cookie cutters from plastic bottles or how to create extra storage from old furniture. Those are life hacks. The point is, you can find "abundance hacks", too.

These hacks exist in all walks of life, and with over seven billion people in this world, it's guaranteed that some have found hacks you'll find useful. Maybe some guy knows how to make awesome money and where to invest it, and has made a video course you're interested in. Another person might know some tasty recipes that will help you lose weight and satisfy you at the same time. (I've certainly found many helpful ones!)

You'll want to focus on how others have grown their abundance. Ask about their experiences. See how they got to where they are today. At the very least, this will help you refine your own plan and move forward, and chances are, they used hacks that you can learn, too.

Unless these people are jerks who don't like to share (or only share for a price), you should glean some valuable intel (and encouragement!) from them. Be interested in their growth and progress, then see if you can apply anything you've learned to your own life. Everyone has a different journey, but no doubt there will be some useful nuggets in there.

(Feel free to write down these ideas in your journal. It's not mandatory, but it'll certainly help.)

Looking at the growth and progress of others is vital in the writing world. Among authors, sharing progress with others (as well as ways to bring in an abundance of readers) is common. Writing the right kind of book is vital, and looking at what successful authors have done gives other authors a general guide to go by. I've read countless success stories and asked my fellow authors about ways to improve my career, which has worked wonders over the years. Doing and paying attention to others' growth gave me the tools I needed to get out of my old job! Years later, I'm still here, enjoying my progress!

Here's your assignment. Whatever you want to attract, there's someone out there who's sharing their growth. Find that person. In the Internet age, there's no excuse. Find that diet blog. Go and do a search for that one on investing. Find a forum about frugal vacations. Go out into the world and find a club who shares your interests. Make some friends.

Aside: *Warning! Warning!* Beware of folks who promise success and make outrageous claims. The world is filled with unscrupulous types, and guess what? They're not truly interested in giving back to others. They only want your money. And worse—the results will almost certainly be crap. How do you spot them?

—They promise or guarantee amazing results and success. (For your money, of course.) Their cleanse will make you drop fifty pounds in a week! Their business kit will make you a millionaire!

—They email you, asking for your business, when you never asked them to and never signed up for their list. Click on their link? Guess what? They want your money! (Even us writers get these. I delete these emails by default.)

—Their website consists of one *long* webpage with loads (and loads) of testimonials that you can't even verify, and nothing else. And at the bottom of the page is the (usually high) price for the abundance they promise. Always do your research!

—They're aggressively pushing their wonder product. You *need* it—and them—for your guaranteed success.

You'll know when you find someone who genuinely wants to share their success and give back. Sure, some of these people might be selling something, such as a cookbook, online course, or a T-shirt, but *they don't promise you a rainbow and a pot of gold just by buying their product.* I've bought some of these things myself, supported these people, and benefited. I once purchased an online marketing course from a fellow author who has given a lot back to the community, and I don't regret it.

Sure, you bought this book, but nowhere did I promise you'd make a million dollars. No one is going to give you what you want in life except for you, but overall, it's way cheaper to do the work yourself, isn't it?

Today I learned!

Did you know that putting yourself in the position of student is just as powerful as making yourself a guru? You can be both—in fact, you *should* be both. With the universe being as big as it is, how can we ever stop learning?

Open up your journal. If you've been doing something to bring yourself abundance every day, then chances are you've learned something new. Maybe it's a recipe, or maybe it's a marketing trend, or maybe it's even a new dating tip.

Let's go back to your rhino repellent. When you first came up with the idea, you went online to see if anyone had made it before. Maybe you learn that no one has made a successful rhino repellent before. Perhaps you learned which parts of the world have rhinos. Whatever. *You learned something.* Write it down.

It doesn't matter what kind of abundance you want. Money? Learn about a new tax break. Learn about how to keep your interest rates low. Research frugal living. (Not too frugal, as you need to live what you want, too!) Love? Learn about body language. Is that person interested in you if they sit cross-legged while you're having a conversation? Writing these things down will not only show you how much progress you're making, but it will help you remember the things you've discovered. These things will add up over time, so learn something new today and write it down.

Still here? Great! I hope by now you've written down some things in your notebook and you're starting to act on them. In the next chapters, we'll get to everyone's favorite topic: money! It's likely that's why you picked up this book.

So, what are you waiting for? Take action. Use your weapons, and start your journey.

Chapter 9: You Might Have More Money Than You Think!

Have you ever met that guy who's always complaining that he's broke? You know the one—his car is always having to go to the shop, he's living on greasy tacos and burgers, and he has a crappy apartment with a dip in the floor that the landlord hasn't fixed. He also suffers from an awful job washing dishes or working in retail. This guy could be a friend, a coworker, a family member, or even you.

Perhaps you've heard, "I'm broke," "I'm stuck here," or some other variant of "I hate my life" that ultimately ties back to money. This guy, let's call him Brandon, doesn't try to find a different job, but prefers to complain about the one he has. Brandon doesn't try to change his diet, yet always complains about headaches, heartburn, and indigestion. As a consequence, he buys weekly boxes of antacids and digestive aids to deal with some... other issues. He's always tired and relies on energy drinks to get through his shifts. Poor Brandon gets home at night and watches some movies on his subscription service to escape from his pain.

Since oil changes and new tires are expensive, Brandon neglects those things. During the winter, he drives to work on roads that are often snowy and dangerous. Since he has bald tires, his car slides into the ditch, ruining his suspension and attracting expensive repairs. If he wasn't broke before, he is now.

And yet, he shows off a new phone he's bought the next day to his friends. They're bewildered, and when one of them points out that an oil change would have been cheaper, he pockets his new phone and asks for gas money. Our guy finds his circle of friends evaporating soon after, and can't figure out why.

Well, when Brandon is telling himself he's broke and that his life is terrible, what do you think happens as a result? His life becomes terrible. If you've read the previous chapters rather than just jumping to the first money chapter, you'll already be able to see the ways Brandon is sabotaging himself and bringing that "I'm broke" mentality to reality. He's attracting disaster and ensuring that he stays right where he is.

(And if you haven't read the previous chapters? Shame on you! Go back and read them so you can understand why Brandon is in the pickle he's in.)

However, a recap might help. Brandon first believes his life can never be better and he will always be poor. He expects disaster (in this case, major car issues) to rob him of his money. Brandon also believes healthy food is out of his reach and too time consuming to prepare, so he relies on unhealthy meals (which causes him to spend more on medicine to make him feel better). Since he tells himself he'll always be poor, he doesn't feel encouraged to find a better job, and so he doesn't attempt to. Even if he does, he gives up quickly *because he will always be broke.*

Brandon's negativity starts attracting bad things to other parts of his life, too, such as his circle of friends. See how he asks for gas money after showing off his new phone? What would you do if a friend did that to you?

By feeling like he will always be broke, Brandon has unconsciously told himself he doesn't have any worth and that he doesn't deserve to be happy or have friends. That's for rich people, right? It doesn't take much imagination to see what this can attract to Brandon's love life as well—or rather, what it *won't* attract.

In this chapter, we're going to go on a journey with Brandon and give him a happy ending. We need to think positive, after all. Let's say Brandon picks up this book (or any other self-help book) and reads it. Maybe he watches some free videos on how to change his life. Whatever. The point is, Brandon has decided it's time to change his mindset, and then takes action to improve his life. (We'll need a few chapters to go on this trip with him since there's a lot to talk about.)

So where does Brandon begin? First and foremost, by looking at his inner world.

Brandon learns where he really stands.

Brandon makes eight dollars per hour at his retail job and sometimes more if he works overtime, which he does during the holidays. When Brandon watches some free online videos about money, he learns that most people in the world make less than he does—far less. In fact, many people in the world live on less than a few dollars per day. Compared to that, eight dollars an hour sounds pretty good!

Brandon looks at his old, small apartment as he reads about people who still live without clean water and electricity. He sees pictures of shacks gathering around cities and sees people wading through mud and trash. Suddenly, the heat coming out of the register doesn't feel so dry and terrible blowing against his skin. The burger he just bought from that place with the scary fast food mascot cost as much as some people make in a day. He's just spent a day's wages on a sandwich he didn't have to pick out of the trash. Brandon runs his sink and pours himself a glass of water, which tastes better than any glass of water ever has. He then checks his bank account to realize he has a hundred dollars—an amount that would take some months to save. For the first time in his life, Brandon doesn't feel so broke. He's actually one of the financially luckier people in the world!

This is the beginning of his journey. This change in perspective is slow, but every time he orders a pizza or buys an energy drink, he sees a full day's wages for someone else exchanging hands. Brandon tells himself that many can't afford an Internet movie service for thirty dollars per month, but he can, and he starts looking for ways to make things even better.

Brandon looks at his money habits.

Since he's paying attention now, Brandon's starting to realize how much he's spending every day on things like junk food and energy drinks. He hasn't really paid much attention to his bank account before, feeling that money is something out of his control. In fact, he dreads it and would rather not know most of the time.

Though it's intimidating at first, Brandon looks at his bank account and adds up the amount he's spending on energy drinks alone. If you've ever bought an energy drink, you'll know they're usually not on the cheap side, and can run to over three dollars per can. Brandon buys an energy drink twice per day, one to wake up in the morning, and one to get through work at night. He realizes he's spending almost six dollars per day for his caffeine boost, and by extension, almost two hundred dollars per month! That's a lot of money he could have for something else, right?

Brandon balks at this amount, and for good reason. But now that he knows about this bad habit, he can do something about it (if only he could find a way to avoid that awful caffeine withdrawal headache).

While looking, he also learns that his Internet movies cost him $360 per year. Fast food alone also costs several dollars per day, and the car repairs came out of some dark hole full of demons. Maybe the new tires, while costing five or six hundred dollars, would have prevented that $1,500 suspension repair bill. Brandon could have had an extra thousand dollars in his account right now!

Knowing where his money goes, and about his spending habits, gives Brandon a sense of power. For the first time, he starts to feel like he can have some control over his finances. But how did he get here in the first place?

Brandon looks at his upbringing.

Brandon grew up to poor parents who had many of the same habits he does now. His parents both worked low-paying jobs, as he does, and struggled to make ends meet. Like him, they also tried to pinch money by skipping important things like teeth cleanings, car repairs, etc. Predictably, Brandon's parents had to contend with expensive dental procedures and even more expensive car repairs. Those are hardly the things that attract wealth. By telling themselves they were poor, they *made* themselves poor. In addition, since everyone needs a way to cope with adversity, Brandon's father turned to tobacco, which, of course, is very expensive, and further tightened the bills.

And what did Brandon learn to do by example? He learned that spending money was to be feared at all times. He learned that the only way to cope with a low bank account was to dull the pain with a distraction. He learned he had to pinch, even when that pinching resulted in more money lost down the road.

It's not as if he decided that he would tell himself to be poor for all of his life. Having grown up around these habits, his subconscious picked up on these cues and told him this was the way he had to live—the *only* way he could live. He grew up believing his story was one of poverty and always would be. He entered adulthood with this mindset and lived accordingly. He would never go to college, get a good job, or do anything great with his life.

Brandon realizes he has worth.

Unfortunately, Brandon spent his life feeling like he wasn't worth much. After all, he didn't have any money, and society had taught him that money = worth. He also lived accordingly, sabotaging himself whenever an opportunity such as a better job came his way, not trying hard enough, and leaving control out of his hands.

Maybe it wasn't his fault he grew up with this mindset?

Perhaps he deserves money and happiness just as much as anyone else!

Of course, Brandon isn't going to go from feeling worthless to feeling like he has worth overnight. Maybe he has to get on some forums and vent. Perhaps he needs to listen to a lot of Internet strangers and take a lot of virtual hugs and kitten pictures before it sinks in. Change is hard, but Brandon slowly embraces it.

Words are power! Brandon seizes the most powerful weapon of all.

A few months down the road, Brandon is almost ready to take action, but there's a bit more work to do.

He has to tell himself that he can turn his life around and not be a broke, friendless, worthless guy.

(Did you catch what was wrong with that last sentence? Thankfully, Brandon did!)

Correction: Brandon tells himself he can have lots more money, better relationships with his friends, and find his worth. Remember, the subconscious takes those negative words like *not* and throws them out, reversing the message, so use positive words instead. See how Brandon saved himself right there? I know I mentioned this before, but it's worth repeating. I definitely felt more positive writing that second sentence over the first.

As a writer, I like the idea that words are powerful. If Brandon tells himself he can be a guy with money, what's he going to do? He's going to look for ways to get himself more money, and many of them are easier than he ever thought possible. You may be getting some ideas on how he can help himself already, and we'll continue Brandon's journey over the next couple of chapters.

Brandon has passed the first part of his journey. He's changed his mindset, and now he's ready to take action, turning his inner world into his outer reality.

Chapter 10: Money Wrangling!

So far, we've seen our friend Brandon really sit down and examine why he's broke all the time. When we started Chapter Nine, we saw that Brandon had a crappy job, small apartment, and a car that breaks down regularly due to lack of maintenance. Brandon lived like this for years, and always just assumed he'd be poor and broke.

Then Brandon looked at his internal universe. There, he was destined to be poor largely because of his upbringing and the programmed stuff he learned while growing up. Turns out Brandon did have some money—not a ton, but some—and he was spending it on things he didn't truly need while neglecting to spend it on stuff he *did*. Once he realized this, he learned that perhaps he could change his situation once and for all. Brandon could get more money if he just made some simple changes to his life.

Now, simple doesn't necessarily mean "easy." It just means *simple* as in "not complex." The great thing about simplicity is that it's not hard to figure out how to do, and if you want something badly enough, such as more money, you'll find a way to make it work. You *can* do it.

When I wanted to up my writing production, I found a simple solution, and it was to do writing sprints a few times per day. This involved having to learn to type quickly with few interruptions—including my cats. If you have cats, you know making a distraction-free environment is *simple*, such as going into a room with a closed door, but not *easy*. Your cat is going to meow, put her paw under the door, and maybe even start chewing on a plastic bag you've left out. You have to learn to tune out the distraction (or just put in some headphones for about an hour).

The same goes for Brandon. He learns that getting more money for himself is simple. Telling himself he can do it is the first—and most vital—step to success and abundance. Great! But what does he do next on his journey to better wealth?

Brandon cuts his costs and hacks his way to more money.

Our friend begins by going through his monthly bills and seeing which costs he can lower. While he doesn't have many bills and doesn't live beyond his means, he has some, and one of the things he doesn't need is his Internet movie subscription. How much does he actually use it, anyway? Brandon only watches one movie per night as escapism.

Cutting this cost is simple, but not easy. Does Brandon have to make his life less fun? Everyone needs to take a break and have fun. That's human nature, and a basic need.

Thankfully, there are almost always hacks to lowering your costs. It's called frugal living. I'm a big fan of frugal living, not because it makes you a penny-pincher, but because it frees up money you can use for other things. There are blogs galore on the Internet about frugal living, and the tips range from how to save on groceries to how to lower your electric bill.

Brandon does some research and discovers he can watch lots of free videos online instead of paying that monthly subscription fee. He can also go to his local library and rent movies for cheap or even free. He can even go to his town's family movie nights, if he doesn't mind sitting on a blanket in the park and watching kids' films. (This is provided nobody thinks he's a creep.)

So, Brandon cancels that monthly subscription by using this frugal hack. He's just saved thirty dollars per month and he can still enjoy movies.

But what about his energy drinks and the fast food he eats?

Brandon decides to tackle this next. There have to be hacks for food, right? He could quit caffeine, but he knows the withdrawal headache is waiting for him. Maybe coffee is cheaper? But the prices at most local coffee shops terrify him even more than the energy drinks do. That's a no go.

Maybe he should buy a coffee maker and brew his own caffeine supply to take to work with him? But that costs money, right?

Well, yes, it does, but maybe we should talk about a concept known as Return On Investment (ROI).

Pretty much everyone who uses advertising throws this term around. Basically, it means what it says—you invest money (or time, or whatever) and get a return on what you put in. This could be more money if you play your cards right. Ideally, you want to earn more money back than what you put in. (This is called a *positive* ROI.) ROI could apply to anything (such as friendship or love) but since this is a money chapter, we'll stick with that here.

When I run advertisements for my books and hope to make more money back than what I spend, that's called hoping for a positive ROI. In Brandon's case, since he's trying to save money, he hopes to *ultimately save more than he'd spend* on energy drinks by investing in that coffee maker.

Brandon is still scared to spend money he doesn't feel is necessary at the time due to his programming from a young age. However, now that Brandon realizes this, he is able to overcome his fear. He buys a coffee machine, reasoning it'll pay for itself in a month or two. He buys coffee, filters, and a thermos so he can port his energy supply with him. This is his initial investment.

After a month, Brandon calculates his new cost for coffee, and it's less than a dollar per day! That's way better than spending six bucks per day on energy drinks. He's just saved another hundred and fifty per month, and in two months, he reasons he'll have saved three hundred. Not bad!

In sixty days, Brandon has already seen a positive ROI. By investing in something positive, he has *attracted more money into his life.*

Now, what about all that fast food? How can he stop spending so much on that?

Brandon turns to a simpler, but scarier hack: he learns to cook. This also requires an investment in pots, pans, a food processor, utensils, etc. But now Brandon knows how this works, and he's willing to spend that money he just saved from ditching the energy drinks to bring himself more money. He learns recipes, cooks himself healthier meals, and packs his own meals rather than buying them. He saves even more money per month, and the effect snowballs.

Remember Brandon's constant heartburn and digestive problems? Now that he's eating healthier, he doesn't have to buy that expensive medicine. Brandon feels better. That's more money saved, and also fewer medical bills down the road.

Brandon starts saving.

Now that he's feeling better about his life, Brandon opens a savings account. He puts a small amount of each paycheck into it. He knows that like all his savings, it will add up. With savings in place, he feels much better at the thought of disaster striking, such as an expensive repair or family emergency.

It's not a ton, sure, but Brandon watches the balance climb every month.

However, after a while, he gets bored with his new saving habit. Instead of going out with friends (now that he's not always asking them for gas money) he's just putting everything into his savings account. Brandon gets more tempted to start buying movies again and to blow his money on entertainment.

Thankfully, he recognizes this and decides to do something about it before it gets out of hand.

Brandon allows a "fun account".

He's already opened a savings account. Great work! But he's decided he has to handle another need: entertainment. As we said, fun is a basic human need, just as food and shelter are. Having an abundance of fun will only bring other things into your life—friends, love, and happiness.

Having all the money in the world is meaningless unless you are able to enjoy your life. That's awfully hard when you're working overtime every night, rise at four AM every morning, and fill your weekends with work duties. Too many people work themselves to death to have money, but never have time to enjoy it. (And did you see the "working to *death*" part?) We've all heard about those eighty-hour work weeks and absent spouses and parents. These people have fallen into the trap of "wanting more" and can no longer appreciate what they have, and loss (such as divorce) usually follows.

So Brandon decides he needs to allow some room in his new budget for fun. Now he can do that! Brandon decides to put all his spare change into his "fun account". Turns out it's a jar on his kitchen counter, but it still counts! It might be a quarter one day or a few dollars the next, but all that change adds up, and Brandon finds he has enough to go out with his friends that weekend. Not only does he blow off some steam and has fun, but he gets to spend time with his friends as well.

Of course, he still doesn't have a ton of money, so he employs a few more hacks. Instead of ordering pizza, Brandon shows off his cooking skills and entertains his friends for almost free.

Brandon decides to finally respect his money.

Before, Brandon didn't care too much about checking his bank account or budgeting. After all, what was the point when he was broke all the time?

Now that he's getting a handle on his cash, he realizes he needs to keep that handle. Brandon knows he can't dismiss the value of his money anymore as he did in the past (without realizing it). Now he knows it's important to respect it, as it's already had a lot of power to change his life for the better. Just learning to handle it better has brought an abundance of friendship and fun into his life. He even enjoys cooking, and can't wait to show off to a potential date.

He respects his money enough to stop wasting it on energy drinks and fast food, which he won't enjoy in the long term. He even respects it enough to know it can take him places—literally. Brandon does what his parents never did: he starts planning for a road trip across the country with his friends. It's not a very expensive trip, but it's certainly a start, and definitely something a "broke" guy would never do.

This means he has to maintain his car and budget money for regular maintenance. Instead of seeing this as a burden, he sees his cash as a means to get him somewhere, literally and figuratively. It's not worth throwing away on Internet subscriptions and unhealthy junk food, and cash is worth earning and saving.

Brandon is sure going far on his journey, but he still has a ways to go before he can call himself "wealthy". In the next chapter, we'll follow Brandon as he continues his trip. He now has some money and good things are starting to happen in his life, but he still has the issue of having a retail job that doesn't pay that much and unexpected bills that pop up from time to time. How does he cope with that? What can get Brandon to the next level?

Chapter 11: Keep It Flowing!

Things sure are looking up for Brandon. He's managed to provide himself with some extra money per month with a few simple steps, and his social life is even on the upswing because of it.

But Brandon's world isn't all rainbows and unicorns yet. He's still working his retail job, and he still doesn't even make double digits per hour. Not to mention that Brandon has also sacrificed some things to give himself a greater abundance of extra money. Does this mean he'll have to pinch pennies for the rest of his life and never do anything that requires a good deal of money, such as go on a cruise? That's not very fun and "abundant", is it? Being frugal is a great way to start getting yourself more money, especially if options are limited at first, but it really is just a tactic to get you to greater things. When climbing a flight of stairs, you don't stop on that first step, or even the second or third.

"I want to cook every meal I ever have at home, stay in my house all the time, and freeze during the winter."

—No One Ever.

Brandon has taken the first steps towards wealth. He had to start somewhere and prove that he could change his life. Now that Brandon's done that, he decides to explore more ways to bring himself more money (and, by extension, an even better social life and greater amounts of happiness). After all, he has a few extra hundred dollars per month to play with now. What can he do with that?

Brandon explores a whole world of possibilities.

Other jobs besides retail exist, and many of them pay better. Brandon gets on the computer and researches a few that interest him. He's always liked manual labor, being handy, and exercising. After all, he used to help his parents fix broken things around the house, so he knows the ropes already.

Brandon looks into a few careers such as plumbing (no shortage of money there!), delivering mail (he could get holidays off!), and even doing odd jobs. Brandon learns what classes he'll need to take to enter the plumbing profession, and while taking extra classes would have scared him before, he knows he has the power to change his life now (and that spending money isn't always a bad thing). He'll have to take out a loan to take his classes, but if he becomes a plumber, he knows he can pay it back.

Brandon invests in some tools he can use for odd jobs. Brandon also offers to fix a leaking toilet for a friend. It can't hurt to practice on something safe, right? By replacing a valve, his friend gives him twenty dollars as a thank you! Now, he's making money back on his investment, and all by putting himself out there.

While doing some odd jobs here and there and putting himself out into the world, Brandon's reputation begins to spread and friends of his friends hire him to fix cabinets, replace sink faucets, and even to mow lawns on occasion. Brandon finds himself earning more and more side money doing something he enjoys, and he finds most toilets more agreeable than angry Black Friday customers. Once he's saved a few thousand dollars (and gone out to dinner at a few fancy restaurants) Brandon applies to trade school. He gets accepted, and starts his classes next month!

Brandon learns to appreciate his ability to pay.

Okay, so trade school isn't cheap, even if in many cases it's cheaper than a college degree. Brandon does have to take out a loan to pay for classes, but instead of bemoaning the price tag, he celebrates.

Since he's gotten his finances under control, his credit score has improved. This has no doubt helped him secure that loan so he can go to school. He also knows that once he enters the plumbing field, he won't have any issues paying it back. Others won't be so lucky.

Instead of complaining, Brandon tells himself there is—or will be—more where that came from. And there will be. The world is opening to Brandon, and it's all because he took those first steps and kept climbing.

Brandon takes small actions to get where he's going.

As word about his handyman abilities spreads through his community, Brandon slowly picks up more and more odd jobs during his free time. (Remember—he's still working his retail job at this point.) Brandon continues to save a bit of his money each month and watch his bank account grow. The same happens for his fun account, and he can even pay for a few dates along the way! He even finds he can once again indulge in an occasional energy drink and buy a meal for himself he doesn't have to cook. After all, Brandon doesn't have quite as much free time as he used to, so he's going to spend it having fun instead of cooking!

He also needs to schedule his classes accordingly once they start. Brandon begins with night classes, taking one or two per semester to avoid getting burned out. Having patience pays off here. He studies one night, does class another night, and rests on a third night. Halfway through his schooling, he realizes his boss is a jerk and won't give him Tuesday off for class, so he takes the leap and changes jobs. Now that he has money saved, he's able to risk the move. Brandon finds a temporary job with a roofing company that pays better, and they hire him because he's given himself some experience with manual labor and can see he's a good worker.

At last, Brandon begins an apprenticeship. He's so close! Working with the roofing company on the side earns him even more experience (and money) while he's an apprentice, and better yet, he likes the people he works with more than he likes toilets. Brandon makes new friends in both fields, builds connections, and gets himself even more jobs. He now has more in his bank account than he's made in his entire life.

At last, he finishes his apprenticeship, gets a degree, and starts his new career as a plumber! Brandon loves the work and starts at a great company that gives him vacation time, benefits, and free training. He still does odd jobs on the side and gets to meet others in the community, and best of all, he meets his wife-to-be on another date!

Brandon learns that sharing is caring.

Now that Brandon has bought his first house, makes enough for a car that doesn't break down every month, and plans to get married, he decides to give back. Maybe he donates to an educational foundation who helps disadvantaged kids. Perhaps he tells his story to others and encourages them to change their lives. Maybe he even writes a book about it (and earns more extra money). He also rests easy, knowing he can support any children if he chooses to have any. He doesn't have to pinch every expense anymore!

And it feels good. He has a dream life, a life he once thought was never possible, and it only promises to get better.

It's time for a review!

Let's say Brandon read this book and took it to heart. Now's a great time to go over the earlier chapters just a little and see how Brandon applied the concepts. (I won't take too long. Promise!)

What power-ups did Brandon use to jump to the next platform? Which mental traits did he work on? Brandon stopped feeling sorry for himself. He also learned to feel joy in the moment, even if he was cooking pancakes for the first time. He also learned patience when he started saving, gained some guts that he used to change jobs, became willing to learn via his classes, craved a new adventure, and decided it's all out there for the taking. And, most of all, he acted on it.

How many of the Five Powerful Techniques can you see in his story so far? If you said, "All of them," you are right. First, Brandon stopped the negative self-talk he learned from his parents. After that, he developed a strategy to attract more wealth (start by saving, go to school, pick up odd jobs, learn, and get a better career). He had other people encourage him and enter his life, he looked to what others had done, and he tackled the changes a little at a time. And look where he is today!

What debuffs did he actively avoid? He stopped letting himself go, which improved his health. This was a side effect of saving money, but feeling better gave Brandon the energy he needed to change his life. Brandon kicked all the excuses he'd ever had to the curb and no longer tells himself he can't afford school. Disaster used to lurk around the corner—*the car might break down again!*—but Brandon now tells himself he's prepared rather than dreading the next car problem. He stopped telling himself he was worthless because he couldn't get more money and, as a result, pulled himself out of the *wanting more* trap.

Which weapons did Brandon put in his belt? He looked at what he was telling himself (he'd always be poor) and examined where that came from. Once he did that, he was able to stop it. Brandon looked at the bigger universe (researching other careers). He gave thanks for the money he'd saved so far, shared his money (going out on dates), became a guru (by chipping away a little at a time at his classes and odd jobs), found hacks others used (by starting the process of saving money rather than blowing it all), and looked back at what he had learned and done during the journey.

Whew! That was a long sentence, and I hope it gets the point across. I'm glad this isn't a horror novel and Brandon has a happy ending, aren't you? He has plenty of cash and now he's much happier than he used to be.

That brings us to the last couple of chapters. If there's anything better than money, it's happiness, and we'll go over some ways to bring more of that into your life.

Chapter 12: Happiness and How to Get More

Happiness is something everyone can get behind, right? We all want to be happy with our lives (whether we admit it or not).

Everyone knows what it's like to be unhappy, even the most sheltered and privileged among us. Even if you have enough money to be very comfortable, maybe you just don't feel that great around your current friends and you find it's a lot of work to keep up appearances around them. What will they think of you otherwise?

Maybe you have lots of friends, but you aren't happy at your job. You get up and go every day to the same boring routine and the same pointless meetings. Working long hours, you never have much of a chance to have any fun, and spend many hours just twiddling your thumbs in your cubicle for the whole day.

Whatever the reason, you've felt unhappy with your life at some point. Depression aside, we've all gone through dark periods, and yes, there are times where it's appropriate to feel under the weather when it's unavoidable, such as suffering the loss of a loved one or losing a job you love. That's normal. I'm talking about the general unhappiness that comes with the lack of abundance in life.

Unhappiness can come from lack of fulfillment at a job. Perhaps it comes from a lack of social activity or a lack of self-esteem. A lack of abundance of many things causes this unfortunate state, but since this is a book about positive thinking and positive action, you may have guessed that there are ways to bring more happiness into your life. You've read about many of them already—how to bring more money, friendship, encouragement, and health into your life. These things can help bring you happiness, but aren't happiness itself.

When you feel better about everything, you're more likely to take the action you need to bring other great stuff into your life, so let's get started!

Be Eager. Don't just dread things and wait.

We've all had that morning where the alarm goes off, seemingly hours too early. Our first thought as we hit the alarm button is probably this: *"Oh, I'm going to have a horrible day at work today. But everyone's right that I need to be practical and stay in a safe job. That's just life. Maybe someday, something cool will happen."*

Think back to the last time you said that to yourself.

How did that day turn out?

Or, if you said that to yourself recently, how is life turning out?

While surprises can and do happen, chances are excellent you had a horrible day at work. Your boss continued to favor your lazy co-worker, you had to stay an extra hour, and your commute involved a traffic jam thanks to a tractor-trailer flipping over on the expressway. Worst of all, you're *waiting*. Not just on the freeway, but waiting for something to happen. Perhaps you're just dreading the next disaster that will cost you cash and staying in your job because of that. Your subconscious knows this, and you feel unhappy as a result.

How could your day have gone differently had you woken up eager to see what the day would bring? How could life go differently if you told yourself that things have to change?

Say your alarm goes off and you think, *"That's one day closer to getting out of this job and commute. One day closer to better things."*

After work you resolve to search for a new job. Maybe you'll write a blog and build your online presence so you can eventually start your own business. Maybe you'll look into investing so you can retire early. How do you think your day and life goes then? Bad things can still happen, but at least you know this isn't all there is. Adopting eagerness will give you the power to take risks and make that leap. Get across that bridge!

I used to be in this position myself. Years ago, I had many of the same problems as the person hitting their alarm in disgust. In fact, I *did* hit my alarm in disgust at five AM every day, commute almost an hour to reach a boring job, and get home late. That was if the roads weren't icy, and if you live in a place that has real winter, you know that's no joke.

Do you know what I did as I worked on getting out of that situation? I got in my car and told myself that this was going to be my last winter doing this crap. And it was, because I was eager to get to my new life and took the risk of switching over to the life I wanted. Had I just "waited" and stayed "practical", where would I be today?

Don't Let the Crab Pull You Back Down!

Once you start making positive changes to your life and step out of your comfort zone, you may notice a phenomenon you've never seen before.

There are people and things out there that will try to sabotage your success. If you've ever tried to lose weight, your friend might have bought you a big candy bar because "We used to eat candy and watch movies together. What happened to the old you?" A sugar craving might have tried to make you give in.

What happens if you give in to your friend? You start eating junk food again and regain all your weight, and now you're unhappy with your progress!

Maybe you wanted to sell your rhino repellent, but your brother tells you it's a dumb idea and you're much safer sticking to a retail or office job, as he has all his life. If you give his words power over your actions, what do you think happens? Your brother now has someone to commiserate with about your awful jobs, and you're unhappy.

Why do people like to discourage? Do others want you to be unhappy?

These people are uncomfortable with your progress because it shines a light on the fact that they haven't taken action to bring abundance into their lives, so they subconsciously attempt to sabotage your progress through "kindness". Maybe your friend who bought you the candy bar thinks she's just being nice and trying to keep your friendship alive. Maybe your brother thinks he's looking out for your safety. This doesn't mean they're bad people. Many don't know yet how to handle change, or even how to make their lives better.

Don't let this discouragement stop you from grabbing what you want out of life. It's a normal part of changing your life for the better, and take heart—if people start doing this to you, you're making progress, even if that's just hatching your idea in the first place.

Beware of toxic people. If someone you're hanging out with always makes you feel tense, sad, or discouraged, maybe it's time to reexamine your friendship. That's not a real friend. (But hey—these people make interesting characters when I write a novel!) That's someone you should consider letting go of.

Find People and Things That Lift You Up.

If you're practicing the techniques in this book, you might have done this already. By giving, whether it's advice or a story, you attract those who want to see you succeed and be happy. People will root for you. Maybe you'll even join a club of like-minded people.

A true friend will want to see you happy. It's *sometimes* necessary to surround yourself with a different set of people in order to change your life. Brandon did this in the last chapters by dating, learning a new trade, and getting a new job. He surrounded himself with people who shared his goals. Maybe you're lucky, you have a great friend like that already.

Maybe what lifts you up is a hobby such as gardening, hiking, or traveling. And if you don't have a hobby or activity that brings happiness to your life? Find one. Do that thing you've always wanted to do, and remember when we talked about not waiting until retirement to do it? Find time, even if you have to turn off the TV for a little while. Break things up. Who knows? You might find you like fishing better than any TV show you've ever seen.

Take Breaks, Enjoy Life, and Goof Off Once in a While.

What? Goof off? But you're trying to *change* your life!

Ever heard of burnout? It can happen even if you're in a career you enjoy. Do something too much and without breaks and you might soon find yourself becoming crabby, tired, and uninterested in what you're doing.

Ever heard the phrase "Stop and smell the roses" or "Count your blessings"? That's pretty much what I'm saying here.

I love writing and telling stories, but I also love being able to take a break on the weekends to goof off, watch stupid videos, or even take a walk if the weather allows. That gives me enough time to be grateful for my working legs and the fact that I can devote my life to doing what I love. Many people don't have these things. Breaks also give me time to be grateful I can work with a purring cat on my lap rather than an awful co-worker.

Without slowing down to enjoy life, I find myself wanting to throw things whenever a formatting change doesn't go as planned. My brain shuts down and I can't focus on what I'm writing. I also schedule my day so I can have evenings off to relax. If I don't, my happiness goes down considerably and I can no longer enjoy what I'm doing. Taking breaks, even a break to lie down and snuggle my cat for an hour, does wonders to put me in a better mood.

Live. Don't just react.

Have you ever just felt like you're going through the motions? Get up, go to work, go to bed, get up, etc.? A pipe in your house bursts. You call the plumber. Then you work to save for the next problem. Ditto. Your roof springs a leak. There goes more money. You stay in your safe job. Drive to work. Come home. Do what the boss tells you to do and adopt new duties without a raise. You're angry. Maybe you watch some TV at the end of each day. The boss tells you to work some new, longer hours, and you do what you're told. Bills go up, so you stay in your boring job.

Going through the motions attracts unhappiness because by just reacting to what happens, you're relinquishing control of your own life to everything else. You're giving control to the company you work for, reacting when things go wrong, waiting for something to happen, and letting your bills dictate what you do with your life.

Imagine that you're proactive instead of reactive. You live instead of react. Since you don't like your office job and know you'd be happy working outdoors, you look into a new career every day and decide to become a park ranger. You act, take the courses you need, and get out of there. Then you move across the country and start working out in the wilderness, and you love it!

Or perhaps you put yourself out there in the dating scene instead of just waiting for someone to notice you. Big difference there, right?

Look at Where You Want to Go.

Would you drive a car without looking at the road ahead?

Okay, okay. Some people really do this. It's downright scary, and we all know it can cause accidents.

When you're not paying attention to where you're going, or if you get into some self-driving car, then you're leaving your destination up to chance. As we've seen throughout this book, that usually doesn't lead to happiness. If you're not keeping a destination in mind, where are you going to go? You might just keep driving down a long, boring road, you might end up in a bad part of town, or you might break down somewhere and find yourself stranded, and since you have no destination in mind, what do you do now?

Let's say you want to go to a party. You want more fun and happiness in your life and all your friends are there. You're not going to just get in the car and go wherever. That's not going to help you reach the party.

When you're in control, you might put the directions to the party into your GPS. Maybe you've written them down if you're old-fashioned.

Life is the same. Avoid driving aimlessly, or worse, making yourself a passenger in your own life. (I once saw a music video about a guy who let a car drive him to random places, and frankly, it was pretty depressing.) Maybe it feels safer to be the passenger—someone else is in charge, after all—but passengers often get no say in the road trip music, the destination, or even the stops. That's always up to the driver, and road trips are way better when you get to do the things you want to do.

In the next chapter, we'll look at the most important aspect of attracting more happiness into your life—you. That's right. *You're* the core of whether you'll attract joy, or go through life miserable.

Chapter 13: You're Worth It
The Ultimate Abundance of Happiness

Okay, I've left the best for last in this book. So far we've talked about bringing more money and happiness into your life, along with an abundance of, well, anything else you could possibly want.

But what's ultimately at the root of happiness?

Mindset, with action.

But what's the most important part of your mindset to begin with?

A good attitude, sure, but what's at the root of *that*?

The answer is simple: loving yourself!

Think about it—if you don't like yourself, it leads to all sorts of awful things: low self-esteem, trying to mold yourself to please others, pinning responsibility on your happiness on others, and, most of all, inaction, and if you've been paying attention so far, you know how that ends.

Realizing you're worth it is so pivotal I have a chapter dedicated to it. Unfortunately, many people believe they aren't worth it. You've likely met people with this problem, and what kinds of lives do they lead? They probably live similarly to how Brandon was living before he started his journey to abundance. Or, if they do appear to have everything on the outside (a nice car, big house, etc.), people who don't love themselves sure don't have an abundance of happiness on the inside. Maybe they have horrible love lives or abusive spouses, or don't have much of a life at all because they don't love themselves enough to escape a bad relationship or a job that forces them to work over eighty hours per week.

See a trend? That's not very abundant, is it? When you don't believe you're worth it, you'll attract what you expect—a lack of love, money, friendship, etc. Thankfully, there are ways to improve this area of your life, and when you do so, all other areas will naturally follow. When you do feel you're worth it, what will you do? You'll likely set out to make your life better.

Be yourself.

Yeah, we've all heard this one. I've even heard a song with this title playing on the radio! It's true—*to an extent.*

Have you ever felt like you have to be a different person around certain friends, relatives, or coworkers? This is a classic case of molding yourself to fit someone else's expectations, and it's not healthy. Years ago, I had to go to work and put on a mask that wasn't me, and you can bet that I wasn't very happy when I was doing it. Sadly, and though I didn't realize it so long ago, I was also fitting the mold that my family provided for me, and that was to work in health care and have a "secure" job. I was, quite literally, working in a job I didn't like all that much to make someone else happy. I was hiding my real self, someone meant to pursue something creative instead, to please someone else.

During those years I had headaches, sleep deprivation, heartburn, digestive issues, and fatigue. Did I mention I hated getting up in the morning? And it was all because I wasn't being myself!

This is a very common problem, and can range from someone giving up a passion to please a group of friends to someone else developing an eating disorder to "fit in" with society. Having to "fit in" leads people to work in jobs they hate and stay in relationships they don't like, all because their family and friends are doing the same thing.

Thankfully, I realized what was happening and got out of the career path I wasn't enjoying all that much! Happiness followed because I decided to be myself, despite discouragement from some people I know. It was liberating!

Aside: Remember that "to an extent" part?

"Be yourself" does not mean you should lie, cheat, murder, and steal because that's "you". What it really means is to be an *improved* version of yourself. If you have trouble keeping a relationship, it may be worth working on a trait that keeps a potential partner away, such as jealousy. If you just can't get promoted at your job, you might want to work on any problems in your performance review. (Or change jobs if your workplace is corrupt and the boss only promotes his family members.) If you need to lose some extra weight, change your diet.

No matter what, you should strive to be the best version of yourself you can be. It may take work, and it's hard to face flaws you may need to work on, but it's worth it in the end. Look at what Brandon did!

Connect and take care of yourself.
Love yourself enough to take care of your health and sanity, and reach out to others when you need to. If you're going through a rough patch, don't go it alone. Even if you have to get

online and join a forum, it's better than nothing. You'll meet others going through the same things you are.

Take the time to research a healthy diet and try to stick to it. Find a good doctor if you need to and are able to. Find a physical activity if you can, which is good for the body and the mind. Taking care of yourself is one of the most powerful forms of self-love. It may be hard at first, but once you reap the benefits, you'll never want to go back.

I experienced this for myself when I completely changed my diet because I decided I deserved to feel good and be healthy, and you can, too.

Be awesome versus being a jerk.

If you've ever browsed the comment sections on news articles and video sites, you've encountered trolls. These people delight in posting mean comments on other peoples' content, or even other peoples' comments. These mean comments range from simple name calling to flat-out racism to insulting another person's religious beliefs (or lack of). Other common troll comments include blaming a victim for something or voicing a very unpopular opinion for the sake of angering others. I've seen it all.

You've also heard the stereotype about trolls: they must be single guys living in their mother's basement who can only feel good by putting others down. While the stereotype is not always true (and not all single guys still living at home are like this), the premise is. Unhappy people like to spread their misery in any way they can, and this doesn't stop at online comments. By not loving themselves or believing they're worth it, the only way for these folks to cope is to bring others down.

And what do these people get for abusing others?

If you answered "true happiness", then you haven't been reading this book. Chances are they won't have any lasting good relationships, good friends, or amazing lives. If they did, they wouldn't be spreading their hate!

How do you combat this? Be awesome online and in real life, and you're far more likely to attract the happiness into your life that the trolls can't seem to reach. Remember the diet blog I mentioned earlier and how Brandon was awesome by helping his friends fix their toilets? By giving to others and offering respect, encouragement, and praise, you'll attract the same in most cases. Just make sure you protect yourself from those who would try to take advantage of you, because people like this are out there. Listen to your gut, and pull away if you find you're giving and giving to someone only to feel drained, tense, and emotional.

Oh, and don't feed the trolls. Nothing makes one angrier than to be ignored. It's hard, but it works, and it's satisfying. They thrive on attracting negative attention. Don't give it to them.

Stop comparing.

Even in my line of work (writing and publishing) it is very easy to compare, say, how many books I'm selling to how many books Author B is selling. This is especially tough for authors just starting out who see others making livable wages while they only sell a few books per month.

All this does is make an author feel inadequate, or worse, over-inflates an ego. Neither is good. One makes an author want to give up, and the other might become complacent, stop learning new things, and fall as times and trends change. Both roads can lead to disaster!

How many people do you know are comparing themselves to the neighbors? *"He has a better house/car/swimming pool than me."* Their coworkers? *"She's making five figures more than I am!"* Even their siblings? *"Dad always favored my brother the best. I must not be worth it."* Comparison doesn't attract happiness. Quite the opposite, in fact. It breeds resentment, which attracts more negative things. Family tension, job sabotage, and more wait.

All comparing yourself to others does is give you a false sense of self-worth. Everyone's journey is different, even if those two people are in the same occupation with similar families and relationships. Life is incredibly complex, and no two people are the same. Comparing yourself to others just makes you focus on someone else rather than on improving yourself and what you're doing. Do this, and you'll free yourself from the comparison trap.

Don't confuse this with learning from others. Learning from what others have done is super valuable and part of improving yourself, but once you apply what you've learned, you'll likely do it with your own twist. That's what makes the journey *yours*.

You have worth! Admit it.

No matter how you grew up or what situation you find yourself in now, know that you have worth. Even if you have to tell yourself that over and over.

Remember how powerful your subconscious mind is? Use it to your advantage here, because if you don't believe you're worth it, how will you ever take action? Start telling yourself you deserve to be healthy, successful, and loved. Do it every day until it sinks in and you're ready to take action, and be careful to avoid using those "not" statements. However you choose to do it is up to you.

You *can* improve. You *can* prove to those who said you can't, or made you feel like you had no worth, wrong. Show them—that's the best revenge. These people have tried to make you miserable because they're miserable. Refuse to let them pull you down. Get out there and grab what you want.

Final Thoughts

Well, that was a ride! I hope you've gotten the point that changing your life for the better is not just possible, it's right out there for the taking— so long as you love yourself, develop the right mindset, and take action. Unless you're a magnet, like attracts like.

Re-read this book if you have to. If you haven't started working on what you want, begin today. In a week's, month's, or even year's time, there will be massive positive change, but be patient. Take risks. Go on that adventure. Make new friends. Give and get back. Do that thing and don't wait for retirement. That's what life is about. It's more than that gray cubicle you hate or that stifling relationship you feel trapped in. Attract what you want. You won't regret it.

Thank you for reading *Go Manifest Yourself: An Abundantly Abundant Mindset.* I truly appreciate you giving my book a chance. If you have any questions, connect with me at my website, www.authordrriley.com.

Acknowledgements:
Special thanks to Torment Publishing! Without you
this book would not have happened. I love you guys.
Thanks to all my family for the support!

Credits:
Jack Llartin - Editor
David R. Bernstein - Publishing & Marketing Support
Jenetta Penner - Publishing & Marketing Support

Made in the USA
Middletown, DE
23 January 2020